KAIZUNO

KAIZUNO

The Proven 5-Step Formula for Success

By
DR. CHRISTIAN FORSTNER
MURAT AYDIN
DR. ROBERT KNOP

THIN LEAF PRESS

Cataloging-in-Publication Data
Names: Christian Forstner, Murat Aydin, Robert Knop
Title: *KAIZUNO: The Proven 5-Step Formula for Success.*

ISBN 978-1-968318-02-4 (paperback) I ISBN 978-1-968318-01-7 (eBook)

Business and Economics, Management, Professional Development
Cover Design: 100 Covers
Interior Design: Dindo B. Sanguenza
Editors: Dhanliza Cellona
Thin Leaf Press

THIN
LEAF

ACKNOWLEDGEMENTS

Writing this book has been an incredible journey; one filled with learning, reflection, and the support of many remarkable individuals. We are deeply grateful to those who have stood by us, offering their guidance, encouragement, and inspiration along the way.

First and foremost, our heartfelt gratitude goes to our families. Your endless love, patience, and belief in us have been our greatest source of strength. Your support has made this journey possible, and for that, we are endlessly thankful.

To our friends and colleagues; thank you for your invaluable feedback, thought-provoking insights, and constant encouragement. Your perspectives have enriched this work, shaping it into something more meaningful and impactful.

We are also deeply appreciative of the professionals and mentors who have guided us throughout our careers. Your wisdom, expertise, and shared experiences have played a significant role in shaping our understanding of business, leadership, and organizational success. Your influence is woven into these pages.

A special thank you to our editor and publishing team for their dedication, patience, and commitment to excellence. Your meticulous work and keen eye have helped bring this book to life in the best possible way.

Most importantly, to you, our readers; thank you for your curiosity, ambition, and desire to grow. You are the driving force behind this book. We hope that the principles and insights within KAIZUNO serve as a guiding light in your journey toward success.

This book is a reflection of the collective effort, wisdom, and shared vision of everyone who contributed. We are honored to share this work with you.

With gratitude,

Christian Forstner, Murat Aydin, Robert Knop

KAIZUNO

THE KAIZUNO TEAM

The three authors of this book are business partners and close friends since many years. They joined forces to write this book together since their talent and experience profiles complement each other perfectly. An outstanding common feature of all three authors is many years of experience in assessing the excellence maturity of international organizations and related consultancy.

Dr. Christian Forstner, the Discoverer

With his scientific mindset, Christian discovered the 5 STEPS many years ago like a natural law of management, during his consulting and assessment work. For over 20 years, he has been using this simple approach successfully to improve a wide range of organizations around the world. The 5 STEPS are now the basis of KAIZUNO.

Murat Aydin, the Implementer

As a strategic management and excellence consultant, Murat has used the philosophy of the 5 STEPS successfully for many years with various organizations. At GC Europe, he implemented the 5 STEPS as the organization's management system, which played an important role in GC Europe winning the Global Excellence Award in 2019.

Dr. Robert Knop, the Transformer

As an expert for seamlessly integrating digital tools with business excellence principles, Robert can transform any level of complexity into playful, accessible user experience. Over the last 6 years, Robert has transformed the 5 STEPS into a unique digital system that allows users to conduct AI-guided self-assessments in only a few hours.

HOW TO USE THIS BOOK

Welcome to **KAIZUNO.**

KAIZUNO is a powerful yet simple approach to achieving **sustainable success** in any field—whether you are an **entrepreneur, a family business owner, a corporate leader, a consultant, a professional seeking career growth, or someone looking to improve the way organizations function.**

KAIZUNO was developed from over 30 years of international experience in managing businesses, improving complex systems, and driving success across multiple industries. What became clear through years of practical application was this: The most effective solutions are often the simplest ones. Instead of relying on rigid, complicated models, KAIZUNO provides a flexible, easy-to-follow formula that works in any organization, industry, or personal development journey. It also works for projects.

For over 20 years, KAIZUNO has been applied successfully in companies large and small, government institutions, small and medium enterprises, and complex projects. It is a proven, practical system—not just a theory. Use this book to both understand the KAIZUNO formula and learn from the examples within the book.

This book is structured in two key parts:

1. **The KAIZUNO Formula**: A step-by-step guide explaining each of the five essential KAIZUNO STEPS.

2. **A Practical Application**: The story of Maya Dani, a hotel business owner who rebuilt her business using KAIZUNO principles. While fictional, her journey serves as a case study to illustrate how KAIZUNO can be applied in real-life situations.

Whether you are managing a business, leading a team, or optimizing your own professional path, KAIZUNO will help you simplify complexity and achieve success with clarity and confidence.

Success isn't about luck—it's about applying the right method consistently.

KAIZUNO gives you a clear, proven roadmap to thrive in business and life. As you read this book, ask yourself:

- How can I apply KAIZUNO principles in my career or business?
- Which areas of my life need more focus and improvement?
- How can I build stronger relationships and long-term success?

By the end of this book, you'll have a practical action plan for implementing KAIZUNO to accelerate your own success journey.

Let's get started!

WHAT IS KAIZUNO?

KAIZUNO is a proven formula to reach success and excellence in a variety of areas of business and life. The formula is explained with information, but this book also reveals how KAIZUNO works in the real world by following the story of Maya Dani, a passionate hotel business owner. She rebuilt her business using the simple yet incredibly powerful KAIZUNO approach, a method that changed everything for her and her company.

For years, Maya struggled with the same questions many professionals face:

- How do I improve my organization without overcomplicating everything?
- How can I achieve real growth while leveraging the right expertise and partnerships?
- How do I create a system that ensures long-term success?

Like many others, Maya had the passion and the vision, but she needed a clear, structured approach to turn that into sustainable success. That's when she discovered KAIZUNO.

This book is not just a theory—it is a real story of how Maya applied this method to transform her business, and how you can apply it in any professional setting, whether you are leading a corporation, managing a small business, or optimizing projects in a larger organization.

KAIZUNO is a 5-step approach to sustainable business success and even business excellence. Let's look at the STEPS.

KAIZUNO: The Proven 5-Step Formula for Success

1. Strive for Success

- Define what success truly means for you and your business.
- Align goals with your strengths, identity, and long-term vision.
- Choose a clear, attractive target that motivates everyone involved.

2. Thrive Through Relationships

- Engage all success-relevant interest groups (customers, employees, partners and suppliers, society, and decision-makers).
- Identify and anticipate their evolving expectations.
- Address concerns proactively to build trust and long-term commitment.

3. Embrace Balanced Planning

- Develop a structured yet flexible plan to achieving success.
- Ensure your plan is feasible, risk-tested, and adaptable.
- Focus on achieving success first, performance second—prioritizing sustainable growth over quick wins.

4. Pursue Practical Implementation

- Build a competent, motivated team that enjoys working together.
- Secure strong partners and suppliers who align with your vision.
- Utilize smart process management, future technologies, and data-driven insights.
- Act with sustainability in mind, ensuring long-term impact.

5. Secure Sustainable Success

- Continuously measure satisfaction across all interest groups.
- Use feedback to refine and improve plans.
- Celebrate achievements while planning for the next phase of growth.
- Future-proof your business by anticipating trends and staying ahead of the competition.

Each step of KAIZUNO ensures that you are not just achieving success today, but securing it for the future... and these simple steps are available to you in this book.

Not everyone wants to achieve excellence. They just want quick-fixes, which may or may not equal long-term excellence. The KAIZUNO method leads to both quick improvements and long-term excellence.

Many entrepreneurs, startup or established business owners, board members or managers just want to achieve quick success. Our KAIZUNO approach is the perfect answer to this request, as the proven methodology always works and keeps working. Even if you just want to improve quickly now, excellence can still be your vision in the long term.

Our KAIZUNO Approach Supports Both Quick Success and Excellence

The key idea of our KAIZUNO approach was: if you define your plan mainly on the basis of expectations of interest groups, you are always on the safe side. While there may be cases of misunderstanding expectations, the general concept of connecting the plan with expectations is a low-risk approach that generates success with a very high probability.

Our KAIZUNO approach is a simple formula that works for any organization, anywhere, regardless of nature, size and complexity.

So, chances are very high that our KAIZUNO approach will also work for YOU.

Table of Contents

INTRODUCTION

KAIZUNO: 5 Steps to Success

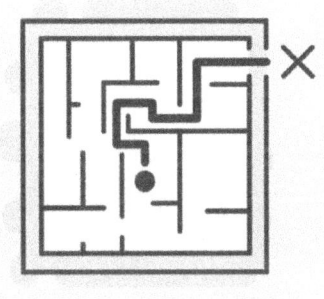

"Success is like following a thread in a maze—you will overcome obstacles and find your way if you stay focused."

—Brian Tracy, Author and Motivational Speaker

While unfamiliar to many, KAIZUNO is not new. It utilizes 5 simple steps for success, and it works for any organization, anywhere in the world. Regardless of nature, size and complexity of various organizations,

KAIZUNO has been used successfully for more than 20 years to create success and even excellence, and it has been used for large global automotive organizations; very large international power-generation industries; medium-size healthcare organizations; international fashion, food and research companies; large oil companies; police and defense organizations; ministries and education institutions; and small- and medium-size family-owned enterprises. KAIZUNO also works for projects.

"Simplicity is the highest level of perfection."

—Leonardo da Vinci, Artist

KAIZUNO is one success solution for many business needs with just 5 simple steps. In a world full of challenges and uncertainties, you need a simple guide to navigate safely through the labyrinth of work and life. Whether it's for private vacation planning or a strategic business challenge, the KAIZUNO systematic approach helps achieve your goals quickly, efficiently, and reliably. Imagine this approach felt as natural as an instinct. That's exactly what our KAIZUNO success-thread offers you.

Global organizations have not only used KAIZUNO but adopted it as their management model. Among them are a famous fashion platform, a global premium car manufacturer, an international hypermarket chain, a global supplier of energy solutions, and a leading oral health company. Although these organizations had their own management systems, they were fascinated by the simplicity of KAIZUNO. Adoption was completely straightforward and the positive impact on their success was obvious.

There is logic behind the KAIZUNO success-formula.

As seen before, the 5 STEPS of KAIZUNO are Strive for Success, Thrive Through Relationships, Embrace Balanced Planning, Pursue Practical Implementation, and Secure Sustainable Success.

The 5 STEPS of KAIZUNO build on each other. You approach them consistently and in the given order, without skipping any single step. You complete each step with care and diligence, and treat all relevant interest groups in a balanced manner. If step 5 does not fully deliver your intended success, review and refine your approach by going back step by step, if necessary.

After each run, you record your success, but also any areas for improvement that need to be addressed. You use this knowledge to constantly improve your organization. In this way, you will become better and better, and systematically increase your success. Only excellence is the limit.

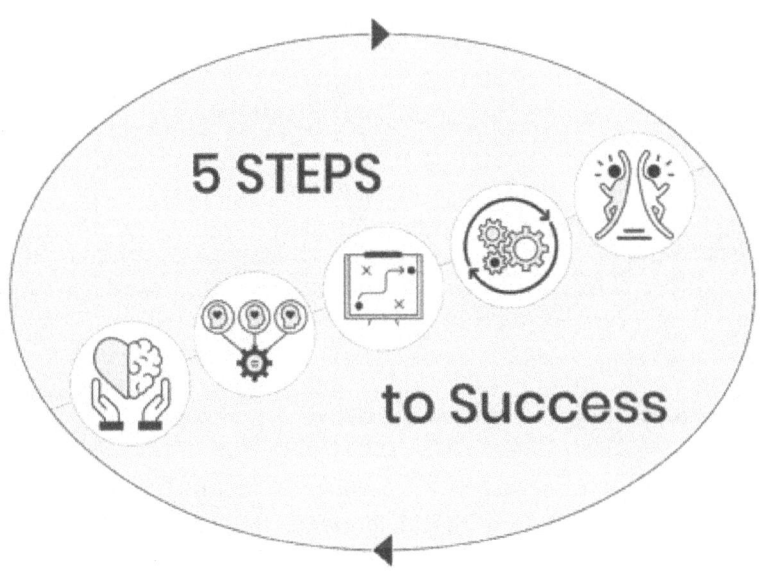

"Life is like a complex network of threads. Success comes when we learn to connect the right threads together."

—Richard Branson, Entrepreneur

If we dig down, it is possible to see many KAIZUNO principles already being used. Examples include the stakeholder-based approach by the World Economic Forum and its sustainable value creation; or Peter Drucker's management approach balancing the interests of customers, employees, suppliers, and communities. KAIZUNO principles can also be observed in our daily life when children play or families plan vacations, where the 5-step model simply creates a vacation that all members of the family can enjoy, regardless of their different personalities.

In the end, the KAIZUNO method is simply great at creating successful solutions for everyone involved.

What Makes KAIZUNO So Unique?

KAIZUNO is unique because of a number of factors, one of which is its natural feel. It is based on a logical sequence that is intuitively applied in many areas of life. These factors were discovered by one of the authors of this book like a natural law, many years ago. His discovery was based on the fundamental insight that complex systems can be most effectively understood, managed, and optimized with simple approaches. As the 5 STEPS are formulated in a logical way, they are not perceived as a set of rules; rather, like a natural flow. They can be quickly understood and put into practice without a great deal of learning. Below are some positive aspects of KAIZUNO.

Strong Focus on Success as a Goal

KAIZUNO is unique because it consistently focuses on success and the concrete achievement of a clear target image. Instead of relying on abstract concepts, the ultimate goal guides action right from the start. The target image is lively and motivating and provides clear orientation throughout the entire process of the 5 STEPS. With this strict focus on success, KAIZUNO unleashes the energy and creative potential of users.

Clear, Active Language and Logical Sequence

The language of KAIZUNO is active and easy to understand. With STEPS such as Strive for success, Thrive through relationships, and Pursue practical implementation, a clear and simple direction is given. All individual STEPS build on each other logically so that you can move from one step to the next with confidence. This sequence creates structure and helps one use time and resources efficiently.

Efficient Through Step-by-Step Quality Checks

Each STEP is completed and checked before moving on to the next one. If success does not materialize as desired at the end of the 5 STEPS, KAIZUNO encourages users to go back and identify the cause. This enables targeted optimization and avoids the risk of carrying problems into later STEPS. The clear sequence and the return approach make KAIZUNO efficient and clear.

Structured and Early Involvement of Interest Groups

KAIZUNO attaches great importance to the needs of all relevant interest groups. Users specifically analyze what is important for every individual interest group, and how diverging interests can be consolidated into a consistent picture. This structured involvement of interest groups ensures that expectations are taken into account before the planning phase starts, which leads to needs-oriented planning and significantly supports success.

Balanced Plan Ensures Balanced Benefit and Success

KAIZUNO ensures that impact desired by interest groups is taken into account during the planning stage. During balanced planning, the expectations of customers, employees, partners and suppliers, society and key decision-makers are translated into a balanced plan, after consolidation to create consistency. This ensures that implementation benefits all interest groups and creates success in a balanced way.

Clear Reflection and Continuous Improvement

KAIZUNO offers a systematic review that specifically highlights what worked well and what can be improved. This reflection is not just a conclusion, but a central component in order to secure findings for the next improvement cycle. KAIZUNO thus promotes a culture of continuous learning and improvement, and ensures that the organization continuously adds value to all interest groups.

Equal Weighting of the Success STEPS

All 5 STEPS are equally weighted since each STEP is equally important. There are no hidden priorities, and all STEPS—from goal-setting to reflection—are seen as equally important building blocks for success. This principle of equal weighting ensures that there are no imbalances or shortcuts on the road to sustainable success.

Equal Weighting of Interest Groups

KAIZUNO ensures that all interest groups are considered equally and without discrimination. By taking into account the needs of customers, employees, partners and suppliers, society and key decision-makers in the same way, KAIZUNO ensures that no group is favored or neglected. This balance promotes fair, holistic development and creates a framework in which each interest group can make its contribution to long-term success.

Universal Compatibility and Adaptability

KAIZUNO is based on simple but powerful universal principles. These correspond to nature as well as to the private and business context. This universal approach makes KAIZUNO fully compatible with a wide variety of models and approaches, which enables the seamless integration of different frameworks. KAIZUNO covers all essential elements for sustainable success and offers a very simple approach to systematic organizational development.

Ariadne's Thread and KAIZUNO

The legendary Ariadne's thread from Greek mythology was an excellent inspiration and role model for KAIZUNO. In the Greek legend of Theseus and the Minotaur, the brave hero Theseus is supported by the beautiful princess Ariadne. She gives him a mysterious thread, the Ariadne thread, to help him defeat the dangerous minotaur in the labyrinth of Knossos.

With the thread in his hand, Theseus ventures into the labyrinth, whose dark corridors lead him into a complex maze of confusion and danger. But he does not give up. Step by step, he unravels Ariadne's thread as he ventures through the dark paths. The minotaur, a terrible monster with the head of a bull and the body of a man, lies in wait for him in the depths of the labyrinth. With a courageous heart and knowing that his only way back is the thread, Theseus confronts the monstrous creature. A violent battle ensues and Theseus finally defeats the minotaur.

The way back is uncertain and full of danger. But Theseus relies on Ariadne's thread to guide him through the labyrinth. **He follows the thread, step by step**, and finally finds the exit. By skillfully using the thread, Theseus is able to escape the labyrinth and return victorious to Ariadne. Ariadne's thread symbolizes not only the way out of the labyrinth, but also the courage, confidence, and determination to overcome obstacles. It is a story of heroic courage and a valuable tool that helps a person find the right path, even in the most difficult situations.

KAIZUNO: There Is No Simpler Way to Success

  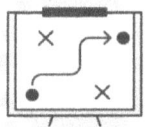  

STEP 1

Strive for Success

STEP 2

Thrive Through Relationships

STEP 3

Embrace Balanced Planning

STEP 4

Pursue Practical Implementation

STEP 5

Secure Sustainable Success

Chapter One

Strive for Success (STEP 1)

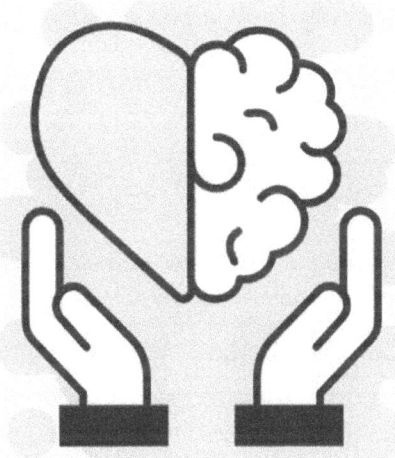

Success needs energy. Without energy, you cannot move forward and every obstacle feels overwhelming.

Motivation is the strongest source of energy. It comes from both mind and heart. When you pursue meaningful goals that align with your values and strengths, motivation drives you forward. The belief that you can truly make a difference pushes you out of your comfort zone and helps you grow.

A clear and inspiring vision channels your collective energy and focuses it on shared goals.

"The mind can tell us what we should refrain from doing. But the heart can tell us what we need to do."

—Joseph Joubert, French Moralist and Essayist

Create Meaning for Yourself and Others

Defining a purpose creates a meaning for yourself and others. This is important for the first STEP in KAIZUNO.

People only do something if it benefits them. They generally tend to make actions that seem meaningful to them in some way, be it through material or emotional gain, security, survival or well-being. This also includes the inner desire to make someone else happy.

Formulating a powerful and meaningful purpose statement requires deep reflection on why your organization exists beyond profit. A strong purpose statement inspires employees, attracts customers, and aligns all interest groups with a common mission.

These are key questions to ask yourself when defining your organization's purpose:

- What meaningful impact do you want to create in the world?
- Think beyond profit: What does your organization want to positively contribute to key interest groups; i.e., to customers, employees, partners and suppliers, society and key decision-

makers? Are you solving a major problem, improving lives, or setting new industry standards?

- Who do you serve, and why do they need you?

Define your core audience and their needs. Are you empowering businesses, improving customer convenience, or providing life-changing solutions?

- What makes you unique in fulfilling this purpose?

Identify what differentiates your organization from competitors. Is it innovation, ethical leadership, sustainability, or customer focus?

- How does your purpose align with your company values and culture?

Ensure that your purpose matches your actions, behaviors, and long-term vision. Do you walk the talk, and do your employees feel connected to your purpose?

- If your organization ceased to exist tomorrow, what would the world lose?

A powerful purpose statement should highlight your unique value proposition in a way that shows your deep relevance. Would customers, employees, or society feel the loss of what you offer? Here are some examples of purpose statements:

DIAGEO: "Celebrating life, every day, everywhere"

THE NEW YORK TIMES: "To seek the truth and help people understand the world"

HUGO BOSS: "We love fashion, we change fashion"

BOSCH: "Invented for Life"

LINKEDIN: "To connect the world's professionals to make them more productive and successful"

"I don't fear the opponent who has practiced 10,000 different kicks once. I fear the opponent who has practiced one kick 10,000 times."

—Bruce Lee, Martial Artist and Actor

When Are You Motivated to Strive for Success?

Imagine you wake up with the morning sun, full of enthusiasm for the new day. What makes those days unique? It is the authentic desire for success that makes the difference.

The desire for success can be found in both our personal and business lives, and often reflects our deepest desires and values. When you really want something, challenges turn into stepping stones, not barriers.

This dynamic is impressively demonstrated in a soccer match in which a soccer team fights on bravely despite falling behind. With every attack, every time they defend the ball, they show their determination. Their relentless pursuit of victory makes every action on the pitch meaningful, and despite falling behind, they turn the game around and celebrate their deserved victory at the end. And this success feels so incredibly good precisely because of the struggle.

A similar spirit of perseverance and teamwork can be found in business life. A highly motivated team in a company cannot be discouraged by setbacks. Their joint experiences include ups and downs, but their coordinated efforts, energy, and belief in success keep them motivated. Each hurdle encourages their creative problem-solving, and together, they finally reach their goal.

However, the motivation for success should go even deeper. If the desire for success is superficial, the effort quickly becomes a burden. It is important to ask yourself: Does your pursuit of success reflect your true values and desires? Because only then will the journey to success be a fulfilling experience.

Part of motivation is keeping a positive attitude, using your strengths, being in harmony with your identity, and pursuing an attractive target. With these things, striving for success can become second nature to you.

Adopt a Positive Attitude

A positive attitude toward the future promotes your resilience and creativity, makes it easier to overcome obstacles, reduce stress, and reach success.

Positive thinking encourages clear decisions and increases satisfaction by focusing on solutions and the wealth of possibilities. You can determine your attitude toward the future by answering the following questions:

- Do you see challenges as opportunities for growth and innovation?
- Do you promote a culture of optimism and determination?
- Do your employees and teams support each other to reinforce a positive mindset?
- Do you set realistic and ambitious goals for yourself and others?
- Do you remain focused and solution-oriented even in difficult times?

How to maintain a positive attitude even in the face of rejection? In the business world and life in general, challenges are inevitable. How you deal with them often depends on your attitude. A positive attitude, shaped by experience and past successes, can make all the difference.

Experience as a Foundation

Our past is full of experiences—both good and bad ones. Every challenge you have overcome, every problem you have solved, has contributed to your resilience today. Even when you thought in the past that "it wouldn't work", you somehow managed it. These experiences form the foundation of your positive attitude, they give you confidence.

Openness as the Key

A positive attitude not only means always seeing the good in everything, but also being open to new approaches and solutions. Openness enables you to think flexibly, adapt and learn from mistakes.

Here are some advantages of a positive attitude:

- Resilience: Remembering past successes gives you the confidence that you can also overcome future challenges.
- Creativity: With an open mindset, you are ready to explore new solutions.
- Stress reduction: A positive attitude helps you focus on solutions rather than problems, which reduces your stress level.
- Decision-making ability: By focusing on what is feasible, decisions can be made in a more targeted manner.

Use Your Strengths

People strive more successfully toward their goals when they are aware of their strengths and use them. This gives them self-confidence as they strive for success.

Self-confidence promotes commitment and perseverance, makes it possible to overcome challenges, and strengthens the ability to find creative and effective solutions to problems.

You can find out how well you use your strengths by answering the following questions:

- Do you make targeted use of your individual strengths to achieve your goals?
- Do you promote the strengths of each team member?
- Do you supplement missing skills through partnerships?
- Do you regularly reflect on your past successes and learn from them?
- Do you focus on continuous training and skills development?
- Do you deliberately use your diverse skills to find innovative solutions?

Why Strengths Are So Valuable, and the "Average Trap" Is So Dangerous

Imagine Wolfgang Amadeus Mozart had concentrated on improving his weaknesses instead of promoting his musical talents. Perhaps he would have tried to become a better mathematician or historian instead of composing symphonies. The music world would be one genius poorer. This example shows impressively how important it is to focus on your strengths and build on them.

The Average Trap

In many societies, people tend to focus on weaknesses. This is often referred to as the "Average Trap". You strive to be average everywhere instead of excelling in one area. But by trying to improve weaknesses, you often miss the chance to recognize and use your strengths.

It is not wrong to work on weaknesses, especially if they get in your way. But it is just as important to recognize where your true talents lie and to promote them.

Recognizing and Using Strengths

Everyone has unique skills and talents. It is crucial to recognize these and bring them to the fore. By using your strengths:

- You increase your productivity: You work more efficiently when you do what you are good at.
- You increase your satisfaction: It feels good to be successful in one area.
- You offer added value: In a specialized world, building on a strength can make you a sought-after expert in that field.

Future-Oriented Thinking

To think future-oriented, you have to go beyond the status quo. Instead of focusing on the here and now, ask yourself where you want to be in five- or ten-years' time. And instead of letting your weaknesses limit you, you should let your strengths guide you.

Be in Harmony with Your Identity

Successful organizations are in harmony with their identity, so this is important for STEP 1 of the KAIZUNO approach.

Your own identity, shaped by your values and your culture, is a central key to success. People strive to act in accordance with their identity, as only this creates a sense of well-being and satisfaction.

From a third-party perspective, a clear identity creates trust, attracts support and respect, and promotes successful relationships and collaboration. A perceived uniqueness then becomes a competitive advantage.

Values are the guiding principles that govern the identity of organizations around the world. Values define the ethical standards and core beliefs that influence decisions, actions and interactions with all interest groups. Clear and meaningful values foster and strengthen a consistent and positive culture.

Values should be defined in such a way that they are in line with the purpose of the organization. On that basis, determining organizational values requires deep reflection on the identity and aspirations of the organization. Here are key questions to guide that reflection:

1. Ethical standards and beliefs

- What ethical principles do you refuse to compromise on?
- How do you define integrity, honesty and accountability within your organization?
- How do you ensure fairness and inclusivity in your decisions and actions?

2. Culture and workplace environment

- What kind of work culture do you want to create and sustain?
- How should employees feel when they are part of your organization?
- What behaviors do you want to encourage and reward?

3. Decision-making and leadership

- What guiding principles should influence your decision-making processes?
- How do you want your leaders to exemplify your values in their actions?
- How do you handle challenges and conflicts while staying true to your values?

4. Customer and interest group relationships

- How do you want to be perceived by your customers, partners, and other interest groups?
- What promises are you making to those who interact with you?

- How can you ensure your values align with and enhance customer trust and satisfaction?

5. Adaptability and growth

- How do your values support innovation and long-term growth?
- How should your values evolve as the organization grows and faces new challenges?
- How do you ensure alignment between individual and organizational values?

6. Accountability and reinforcement

- How do you measure whether you are living up to your values?
- How do you embed your values into daily operations and company policies?
- How do you ensure that employees at all levels uphold these values?

Here are some examples of value statements:

BMW: "Responsibility, appreciation, transparency, trust and openness"

MICROSOFT: "Respect, integrity, accountability"

SIEMENS: "Excellence, innovation, responsibility and integrity"

PATAGONIA: "Quality, Integrity, Environmentalism, Justice and Not bound by Convention"

EUROPEAN INVESTMENT BANK: "Integrity, Respect, Cooperation, Commitment and Equal Opportunities"

Why Identity-Creating Work Is So Important

In an old corner store, between creaking floorboards and the smell of coffee, you could feel the essence of identity. Every conversation, every object is a reflection of the people and their history.

In today's digital age, where screens and algorithms dominate, we ask ourselves: where is the real, the personal? Our identity is not only an anchor in the analog world, but also in the digital space. It gives us stability, orientation, and uniqueness.

People have a deep desire to act in harmony with their identity. Acting against your own identity and finding yourselves in environments that are not in line with your values can lead to dissatisfaction and discomfort. Striving to be authentic and making decisions in line with your identity is key to personal well-being.

While the way we communicate and interact is changing in the digital world, the core of our identity remains constant. It tells the story of our lives, our dreams, and our values. In both the analog and digital worlds, it is our identity that defines us and sets us apart from others. It is the timeless element that offers stability in an ever-changing world.

In a market that is flooded with offers, identity is becoming a decisive competitive factor. It emphasizes uniqueness that differentiates us from the masses. In a world where products and services often seem interchangeable, it is identity that attracts and retains customers. It is this unmistakable personality that creates trust and emphasizes the true value of an offer.

Pursue an Attractive Target that Appeals to Everyone

An attractive target acts like a magnet: It stimulates and inspires all interest groups, bundles energy, and promotes alignment toward common goals. If you imagine that attractive target to be 5-10 years in the future, you may call it your vision.

A shared vision motivates, overcomes obstacles, and creates a clear target for the path to success, like a North Star. It provides orientation and encourages continuous commitment.

A good vision is a short statement that is highly attractive for your people, customers and all other interest groups. It paints a desirable picture of success and motivates everyone to strive toward it.

It should be ambitious but also realistic and achievable, much more than a dream. Thereby, a good vision challenges your organization to stretch beyond its current capabilities and strive toward something greater.

A good vision is fully in line with purpose, identity and values. Together, these four elements create the overarching framework for all organizations. Everything else is inside this framework and governed by it.

You want to craft a clear, inspiring, and desirable vision that acts like a guiding force, a North Star and a magnet for long-term success. Then these key questions might help you:

Future aspirations

- Where do you want to be in 5-10 years?
- What does long-term success look like for you?
- If you achieved everything you aimed for, how would the world be different?
- What would you be most proud of accomplishing?

Relevance and alignment of interest groups

- How does your vision inspire and align employees, customers, partners and suppliers, society and key decision-makers?
- How does your vision address evolving market trends and customer needs?
- How can you ensure that your vision stays relevant and meaningful over time?
- What values and principles must guide you toward this vision?

Competitive positioning and differentiation

- What do you want to be known for?
- How do you differentiate yourselves from competitors?
- What unique strengths and capabilities will help you achieve this vision?

- How can you become a leader or pioneer in our field?

Achievability and strategic feasibility

- Is your vision ambitious yet realistic and achievable?
- What major obstacles could stand in your way?
- What bold steps must you take today to move toward your vision?
- How will you measure progress along the way?

Sustainability and long-term impact

- How do you ensure that your vision contributes to a sustainable future?
- What role do environmental, social, and governance (ESG) factors play in your long-term goals?
- How do you balance growth, innovation, and responsibility?

Internal culture and motivation

- How can your vision energize and inspire your teams?
- How do you ensure that every employee understands and embodies this vision?
- What kind of leadership and culture will you need to cultivate to make this vision a reality?

Here are some examples of vision statements:

NORWAY: "A sustainable, green and climate-neutral society by 2030"

WWF: "Building a future in which people live in harmony with nature"

NIKE: "Bring inspiration and innovation to every athlete* in the world"

*If you have a body, you are an athlete.

IKEA: "To create a better everyday life for the many people"

NETFLIX: "Becoming the best global entertainment distribution service"

What Makes Your Target Image Useful and Attractive?

In order to implement your plan effectively, a clear target image is essential. While the vision is the short statement, so that everyone can easily remember it, the target image is a more detailed version of that vision.

The target image outlines a clear imagination of the future direction. It serves as a motivating and inspiring concept and acts as a guideline for the development and realization of your plans. Like the vision, the target image is designed for the long term and typically covers 5 to 10 years into the future.

"A pile of stones ceases to be a pile of stones as soon as a single person looks at it, carrying the image of a cathedral within them."

—Antoine de Saint-Exupéry, French Writer and Pilot

Still, the target image should never be carved in stone. Internal or external disruptions may require adjustments. Examples could be the COVID-19 pandemic or sudden political disruptions on an enormous scale. The timely adjustment of the target image is a key success factor for organizations.

The Pursuit of Excellence Is Timeless

On the bottle of Kikkoman soy sauce, the label proudly states, "Over 300 years of excellence". Excellence is a particularly challenging version of a vision and the associated target image. It defines a hypothetical state in the future when all stakeholders are fully satisfied. While this target will never be achieved in reality, it can still be an aspiration of very ambitious organizations.

Although the concept of excellence has traditional roots, its core philosophy is timeless and remains relevant in today's fast-paced business world. Here are some reasons why it is still relevant today.

Organizations that foster a culture of excellence are better prepared to change quickly and adapt to new market trends, technologies, and consumer preferences. This can be a competitive advantage in today's dynamic world.

The pursuit of excellence promotes a culture of continuous improvement and innovation. At a time when the nearest competitor is just a click away, the ability to constantly improve and reinvent becomes a matter of survival.

While most organizations seek quick wins—since they are judged by short-term success—instead of taking the long road to excellence, the fundamental principle of striving for the best can be a stable backbone for sustainable success.

Bridging Theory to the Story of Maya Dani

The principles of structured success and excellence are not just theoretical ideas—they have real impact when applied. While every organization faces unique challenges, the fundamentals of KAIZUNO remain the same.

To illustrate how these principles come to life, let's step into the journey of Maya Dani—a visionary entrepreneur who transformed a failing business into an industry leader. Her story is not just about rebuilding a hotel; it is about embracing change, overcoming obstacles, and applying KAIZUNO to create lasting success.

On 12 February 2025, the event host's voice thundered through the grand ballroom, but for a split second, I couldn't hear a thing. A hundred eyes stared up at me. Some were expectant, some skeptical. A few were checking their phones.

I swallowed hard. The heat of the spotlight burned against my skin as the introduction came.

"Ladies and gentlemen, please welcome the visionary entrepreneur behind one of the most innovative hotels in the industry—Maya Dani!"

Applause rolled through the crowd as I stepped forward, my heels clicking against the polished wooden stage. I took a deep breath, fingers tightening around the microphone.

"Fifteen years ago, I stood in front of a crumbling, forgotten building with a rusted key in my hand and a dream so fragile it could break. Back then, I wasn't a hotelier. I wasn't even sure I would survive the first year. Tonight, I stand before you as the founder of Hotel Mirabelle."

A soft murmur rippled through the crowd. They were interested.

"The journey wasn't easy. In fact, it almost ended before it began. I faced setbacks that nearly broke me, decisions that kept me up at night, and moments where I doubted everything. But through every challenge, one thing kept me moving forward—a structured approach to success. Not luck. Not guesswork. A clear, step-by-step process that allowed me to navigate uncertainty and build something sustainable."

I paused, letting the anticipation settle.

"Today, I want to share that process with you. Because success—whether in business or life—is not just about ambition. It is about clarity. It is about knowing what truly matters, involving the right people, planning wisely, executing relentlessly, and ensuring what you build can stand the test of time."

I leaned forward slightly, locking eyes with the audience.

"So let me take you back to where it all began—the day I walked into that old building and made the decision that would change my life forever."

With that, I stepped back from the microphone, and the screen behind me lit up with the first chapter of my story—how Mirabelle was born.

Strive for Success (STEP 1) - Application

Create Meaning for Yourself and Others

December 12, 2009, was the first time I stepped into the building that would become Mirabelle; I nearly turned back. The air was thick with dust, the kind that made every breath feel like swallowing history. A single light flickered in the empty lobby, casting eerie shadows against peeling wallpaper.

The scent of mildew clung to the walls, mixing with the faint, sour odor of something long abandoned. I ran my fingers over the wooden reception desk—once elegant, now scarred with cigarette burns. This wasn't a hotel. It was a graveyard of failed dreams. What was I thinking?

I gripped the cool, rusted metal of the key in my palm, as if squeezing it could stop the wave of doubt rising inside me. Then, out of nowhere, I heard my father's voice in my head, "If you wait for the perfect moment, you'll wait forever. Start now, figure it out later."

I let out a shaky breath. This place was broken. But maybe, just maybe, so was I. And maybe, just maybe, we could rebuild each other.

The building before me was old, neglected, and far from the boutique hotel I had envisioned. The walls carried years of dust and forgotten stories; the windows fogged with time. It was hard to imagine that one day, guests would walk through its doors and feel at home.

But deep down, I knew that this place could become something special. I didn't just want to run a hotel. I wanted to create an experience, a space where travelers felt a sense of belonging, where every guest left with more than just a good night's sleep—they left with a story.

But before I could create meaning for others, I had to find my own purpose in this journey.

Finding My Why

As I stood in the empty lobby, I asked myself: *Why does this matter to me? Why will it matter to others?*

At first, the answers weren't obvious. I had inherited this building from my parents, but it wasn't just about carrying on a family legacy. It wasn't about money either—if it were, I would have sold the property and moved on.

Then, the memories started coming back. I thought of all the times I had traveled and stayed in hotels that felt cold and transactional, where no one truly cared who I was or why I was there. I remembered the exhaustion of business trips, the loneliness of unfamiliar cities, and the moments when I wished a hotel was more than just a room with a bed—I wanted it to feel like a place where I belonged.

That's when I knew. I didn't want to just manage a hotel—I wanted to build a space that gave people the warmth, care, and comfort they didn't know they needed.

But this wasn't just about guests.

For travelers, Mirabelle had to be a home away from home.

For employees, it had to be a place where they felt valued and empowered.

For partners and suppliers, it had to be a hub that supported local artisans and businesses.

For society, it had to contribute to the local culture and community.

For key decision-makers, it had to be a sustainable, innovative model of hospitality.

I realized that success wasn't about running a hotel—it was about creating a meaningful experience for others.

Creating Meaning for Others

When I found my *why*, I wanted to focus on things outside of me. I envisioned a place where:

- Travelers felt at home, no matter where they came from.
- Local artisans, chefs, and creators had a platform to share their craft.
- Employees weren't just staff but valued members of something bigger.

I didn't want Mirabelle to be just another boutique hotel. I wanted it to be:

- A community-driven space that reflected the city's culture.
- A place where service felt deeply personal, not just professional.
- A haven where every guest felt like they belonged.

At that moment, I defined my purpose—not just for myself, but for Mirabelle: To create a home away from home where travelers find connection, comfort, and a sense of belonging—while supporting the local culture and community.

That meaning became my North Star. And from that moment, every decision I made—from how we designed the rooms to how we trained our employees—had to align with that vision.

What If Mirabelle Disappeared?

One night, as I stood in the lobby, I asked myself the ultimate question: *If Mirabelle disappeared tomorrow, what would the world lose?* Would it be just another closed business? Another forgotten name?

Or would it leave a real void?

Would travelers miss a place where they truly felt welcomed and cared for?

Would employees miss working in an environment that valued and empowered them?

Would local businesses lose an important partner that showcased their craft?

Would the community lose a space that added warmth and culture to the neighborhood?

I wanted the answer to be *yes*. Mirabelle had to stand for something more than just hospitality. It had to be a place where every person who walked through the door felt a part of something meaningful.

This was bigger than a hotel—it was a movement.

And I was ready to bring it to life.

Adopt a Positive Attitude

I stared at the laptop screen, my heart pounding: Guest Review: 2 Stars

"It's a nice concept, but it doesn't feel special. The rooms are plain. The service is polite, but forgettable. It's just... fine."

Fine.

Fine was worse than bad. A bad hotel could be fixed. A forgettable one? That was a death sentence. My stomach twisted as I clicked through the reservations calendar. Cancelations. Empty weekends. Rent was due in five days. Employee salaries in ten. I pushed back from my desk and ran a hand through my hair. The weight of exhaustion pressed against my skull.

I had thrown everything into Mirabelle. And right now, it felt like it was slipping through my fingers. I needed to fix this. Fast. I closed my eyes, letting the frustration settle, but then a memory surfaced. I was 18, working my first job at a small café. My boss, Mr. Leclerc, was a perfectionist. Every espresso shot had to be timed, every plate had to be arranged with care.

One evening, I spilled an entire tray of cappuccinos on a customer. Humiliated, I braced for a lecture. Instead, Mr. Leclerc handed me a towel and said, "The only people who never make mistakes are the ones who never try. The trick is to learn fast."

That lesson stuck with me. Mirabelle wasn't failing—it was learning.

Seeing Challenges as Opportunities

The next morning, I walked through the hotel as if I were a guest, seeing it through fresh eyes.

- The rooms were clean—but lifeless.
- The hallways were quiet—but cold.
- The service was efficient—but impersonal.

I knew what I had to do. By nightfall, I gathered my team.

"We are not running a hotel," I told them. "We are creating an experience. We are giving people a story."

I picked up a marker and scrawled three words on the whiteboard:

Warm. Personal. Unforgettable.

"From now on, every decision, every interaction, every detail—it has to make our guests feel like they belong here."

From these early days of Mirabelle, I quickly learned that the difference between success and failure wasn't just planning—it was mindset.

Choosing Progress Over Perfection

Lesson #1: Experience Builds Confidence

I realized that focusing on what was going wrong was only going to hold me back. Instead, I trained myself to see progress, not just problems. But I didn't just develop this attitude overnight. It was built from my past experiences—every challenge I had already overcome.

When I spilled cappuccinos as a teenager, I learned that mistakes are part of learning.

When I faced my first financial struggles, I learned that every problem has a solution if I stay focused. And now, when faced with a negative review, I realized that this was simply another moment to grow, not give up.

- Instead of seeing this as failure, I looked for the opportunity.
- Instead of obsessing over low bookings, I celebrated every single new guest who walked through our doors.
- Instead of stressing over imperfections, I focused on small daily improvements.
- Instead of seeing mistakes as setbacks, I saw them as lessons guiding me forward.

One day, after receiving a negative review from a guest who found our rooms "too simple", I felt disheartened. But instead of dwelling on it, I asked myself: "What can I learn from this?"

That review led us to redesign the rooms slightly, adding thoughtful touches: Warmer lighting, locally crafted décor, handwritten welcome notes.

Weeks later, another guest praised the atmosphere, calling it *a perfect blend of simplicity and warmth.*

That's when I realized: A positive attitude isn't about ignoring problems—it's about using them to grow.

Leading with Optimism

Lesson #2: A Leader's Attitude Shapes the Culture

It happened at the worst possible time—peak breakfast hours. A full house. And the damn coffee machine died. The line at the restaurant counter grew by the second. Guests murmured, some glancing at their watches, others frowning at their empty mugs.

I saw one man checking his phone, about to post a complaint online. Panic clawed at my chest, but I forced a smile. I walked up, not with an apology—but with an idea.

"Alright, everyone," I announced, clapping my hands. "Change of plans! Instead of waiting for a machine, we are bringing in fresh coffee from the best café in town."

Surprised glances. Curious whispers.

"And while we wait, we are doing something special. We are turning this into a coffee-tasting experience—five different blends, all sourced from our favorite local roasters."

Silence. Then laughter. Then… applause.

An hour later, the crisis was a social media sensation. Guests posted photos of their 'surprise coffee-tasting' experience. "Best hotel ever," one wrote. "Where else does a broken coffee machine turn into a coffee adventure?"

That night, I leaned against the counter, watching the buzz in the restaurant. The crisis was not averted. No—it was transformed. That day, I saw firsthand how a leader's energy sets the tone for an entire business. If I had panicked, employees would have panicked. If I had shown frustration, they would have absorbed that stress. But because I chose to approach the problem with positivity and creativity, my team followed suit.

That was the moment I understood: Leadership isn't just about solving problems—it's about how you approach them.

Final Lesson: Positivity Creates Possibilities

Looking back, I realize that Mirabelle didn't survive because everything went smoothly. It survived because I chose to see opportunities in every challenge.

A positive attitude doesn't mean ignoring reality—it means believing that:

- No obstacle is permanent.
- Every problem has a solution.
- Even the hardest days are part of the journey.

Customers felt the difference when they were welcomed with warmth and attention to detail.

Employees felt valued because they saw problems as opportunities, not disasters.

Partners and suppliers appreciated working with a business that focused on solutions, not complaints.

Society appreciated a business that treated guests, employees, and the community with respect and care. Key decision-makers saw the resilience and innovation that set Mirabelle apart. And that's how Mirabelle turned from a struggling business into a place where people from all over the world come to feel at home. Because, in the end, it is not just about building a hotel—it is about building a mindset that sees possibilities everywhere.

Use Your Strengths

When I started Mirabelle, I made a mistake that nearly cost me everything—I tried to do everything myself. I believed that to be a successful entrepreneur, I had to master every part of the business:

- Marketing
- Operations
- Finance
- Guest services
- Employee training

I worked long hours, trying to become good at all of it. But instead of excelling, I found myself stuck in the average trap. I was spreading my energy too thin. I was competent in many areas—but exceptional in none. I was exhausted, overwhelmed, and making slow progress.

Then, one day, I sat in my office, staring at another mistake on a financial report. The numbers weren't adding up, and my frustration boiled over. "I don't understand this. I should be better at this."

Daniel, my operations manager, glanced at me and said something that changed my perspective forever: "Maya, you don't have to be great at this. You just have to know someone who is."

That's when I realized something important: The most successful businesses don't rely on one person doing everything—they rely on people playing to their strengths.

Escaping the Average Trap

I took a step back and asked myself:

- What am I naturally great at?
- What do I love doing?
- Where do I bring the most value?

After deep reflection, I identified my superpowers:

- I understood people. I could read emotions, anticipate needs, and build relationships effortlessly.
- I was creative. I had an eye for detail and loved designing unique guest experiences.
- I could inspire. I knew how to motivate my team, making them feel valued and driven.

Instead of wasting time forcing myself to be great at spreadsheets, I leaned into my strengths—and everything changed.

Delegating My Weaknesses

Once I focused on what I did best, I needed people who could complement my weaknesses.

- Finance and Operations—I hired Daniel, a hotel operations expert, to handle the numbers and efficiency.
- Marketing and Sales—I partnered with Lena, a branding strategist, to manage social media and outreach.
- Culinary and Service Excellence—I empowered Luis, my head chef, to take full ownership of the restaurant experience.

The result?

I had more time to focus on creating memorable guest experiences. My team felt empowered and trusted. The business ran smoother because each person was playing to their strengths.

I had escaped the average trap. Instead of trying to be competent in everything, I built a team where each person was excellent at something.

Turning Strengths into a Competitive Advantage

By focusing on what I did best, I made Mirabelle stand out from other hotels.

- I used my creativity to design small, personal touches— handwritten welcome notes, locally inspired room décor, and personalized recommendations.
- I used my ability to connect with people to build long-term relationships with guests, employees, and partners.
- I empowered my team to take ownership, making Mirabelle feel like a shared vision, not just a business.

One day, a guest told me: "Your hotel feels different—like someone actually cares about the experience, not just the business side."

That's when I knew—I had finally built something unique, something that couldn't be copied.

Future-Oriented Thinking: Strengths as a Long-Term Success Factor

One evening, as I reviewed our guest feedback, I realized something: Playing to my strengths wasn't just about surviving—it was about shaping the future.

My creativity could continue shaping new guest experiences year after year.

My ability to connect with people would strengthen long-term relationships with guests, employees, and partners.

My team's expertise would continue growing as I empowered them to lead in their areas.

Instead of worrying about everything I wasn't good at, I focused on what I could build on. And I started asking a bigger question: "Where do I want Mirabelle to be in five years? Ten?"

The answer wasn't about fixing my weaknesses—it was about doubling down on my strengths and surrounding myself with people who complemented them. That's how I knew: This was just the beginning.

Final Lesson: Your Strengths Are Your Superpower

Most people waste time trying to fix their weaknesses instead of leveraging what makes them great. I learned that the key to success isn't being great at everything—it's being exceptional at a few things and surrounding yourself with people who complement your skills. When I focused on strengths:

- Customers felt the difference when they were welcomed with warmth and attention to detail.

- Employees felt valued because they were trusted to play to their strengths.

- Partners and suppliers saw the value of working with a business that embraced its unique strengths.

- Society benefited because Mirabelle supported local artisans and culture.

- Key decision-makers recognized that long-term success is built on strong, specialized teams.

That's how Mirabelle became more than just a hotel. It became a place where everyone—guests, employees, and even I—could thrive by doing what they do best.

Be in Harmony with Your Identity

In the first year of Mirabelle, I made one of the biggest mistakes an entrepreneur can make—I tried to be everything to everyone. I wanted to attract business travelers, backpackers, luxury guests, and families all at once. I thought that the broader my appeal, the more successful I would be.

But instead of attracting more guests, I confused them. Some people expected a high-end experience, while others looked for budget-friendly stays. Some wanted a quiet retreat, while others sought a lively social atmosphere.

No one really knew what Mirabelle stood for—and honestly, neither did I. That's when I realized: If I didn't define my identity, the market would define it for me.

Defining Who We Are

I took a step back and asked myself:

- Why did I start this hotel?

- What experience do I want guests to have?

- What makes Mirabelle different from other hotels?

The answer became clear. Mirabelle wasn't a five-star luxury hotel. It wasn't a budget stay. It was a warm, personalized boutique hotel for travelers who valued authenticity, comfort, and connection.

I wasn't just running a hotel—I was creating a home away from home for people who wanted meaningful travel experiences. But defining an identity wasn't enough—I needed a foundation for every decision moving forward.

One evening, after reading yet another review saying, *Nice hotel, but nothing special*, I gathered my team. "We need to decide what Mirabelle truly stands for," I told them. Together, we wrote down the core values that would guide every choice we made.

Our Identity Through Values

Rather than just winging it, we created a structured value system.

Mirabelle's values:

Authenticity—We create genuine experiences that celebrate local culture.

Warmth and Connection—Every guest should feel like they belong.

Excellence in Service—Every detail matters; we go the extra mile.

These weren't just words on a whiteboard. They became the DNA of Mirabelle. Every value had to be reflected in our actions—our leadership, decision-making, and relationships with customers, employees, partners, and society.

We asked ourselves the key questions that would keep us in harmony with our identity:

- Ethical Standards and Beliefs—How do we ensure fairness, integrity, and trust?
- Culture and Workplace—What kind of environment do we want for employees?

- Decision-Making and Leadership—How do we make choices that stay true to our values?

- Customer and Interest Group Relationships—How do we ensure that guests feel connected to Mirabelle?

- Adaptability and Growth—How do our values help us evolve over time?

- Accountability and Reinforcement—How do we measure whether we live up to our values daily?

Once we committed to these values, everything changed.

Aligning Every Decision with Our Identity

Once I embraced who we truly were, everything became clearer and easier.

- Interior Design—Instead of generic hotel décor, we used locally crafted furniture, warm lighting, and natural textures to create a cozy, welcoming space.

- Guest Experience—We focused on thoughtful hospitality— personalized welcome notes, curated city guides, and warm interactions instead of impersonal service.

- Marketing and Branding—We stopped trying to appeal to everyone and started targeting travelers who valued intimate, culture-rich stays.

And something incredible happened—the right people started finding us. We began attracting guests who loved the experience we offered, and they became our biggest advocates.

Saying No to Stay True to Ourselves

Once we found our identity, we had to protect it—which meant learning to say no.

- We didn't compete on price. If someone wanted a budget stay, we weren't the right fit.

- We didn't compromise on quality. If a supplier's values didn't match ours, we found someone else.

- We didn't overextend. Instead of chasing every trend, we focused on what felt right for our brand.

One day, an investor approached me with an idea—turn Mirabelle into a chain. The idea was tempting. Growth, expansion, more revenue. But as I listened, I realized something—he wanted to scale the business by cutting costs, streamlining operations, and removing the personal touches that made us special.

It would have made us just another hotel. So I said *no*, because staying true to our identity was more important than chasing growth at the cost of what made us different.

The Toughest Decision—Leading with Integrity

One morning, my assistant, Ana, walked into my office, looking troubled. "Maya, we have a problem. One of our front desk employees, Ben, has been receiving complaints. Guests say he's dismissive and unhelpful."

Ben had been with us since the beginning. He was hardworking but struggled with guest interactions. I sighed. "Do you think he can improve?" I asked.

Ana hesitated. "Maybe. But at this point, it's hurting our reputation."

This was one of those defining leadership moments. Our values weren't just words on a page. If we believed in warmth and connection, we couldn't tolerate poor service.

I called Ben in for a conversation. "Ben, I appreciate your hard work, but hospitality is about people. Guests need to feel welcome. I want to support you, but we need to see real improvement."

He nodded, but in the following weeks, nothing changed. I had to make the tough call. Letting Ben go wasn't easy, but leaders must make decisions that protect the identity of their organization. And in the end, our guests—and our team—felt the difference.

Final Lesson: Own Your Identity, or Others Will Define It for You

Mirabelle succeeded not because we tried to be everything to everyone— but because we became the best version of ourselves.

- We knew who we were.
- We designed everything around that identity.
- We protected it, even when tempting opportunities came along.

And because of that, our guests didn't just stay with us—they connected with us. That's how we built a brand that people trusted, loved, and returned to.

Pursue an Attractive Target that Appeals to Everyone

When I first launched Mirabelle, I had one goal: fill every room, every night. I thought that as long as we had guests, we were on the path to success. But I quickly realized that chasing every possible guest wasn't a plan—it was a recipe for confusion.

Some travelers wanted luxury, while others wanted affordability. Some looked for business amenities, while others sought adventure. Trying to appeal to everyone meant I wasn't truly attracting anyone. I needed to shift my focus.

That's when I asked myself:

- Who is the ideal guest for Mirabelle?
- What do they truly want?
- How can I create an experience they won't find anywhere else?

The answer wasn't about targeting everyone—it was about creating an experience that felt irresistible to the right people.

Defining a Clear and Inspiring Vision

One evening, I sat down, reflecting on where I wanted Mirabelle to be in five years. I wrote down our vision statement: "To be the most beloved boutique hotel for cultural explorers, offering unique, immersive travel experiences that make every guest feel at home."

This wasn't just an idea—it became our North Star.

A strong vision had to:

- Align with Mirabelle's purpose, identity, and values.
- Be ambitious but achievable.
- Motivate employees, guests, and partners.
- Stand the test of time, while allowing flexibility for adaptation.

Now, every decision—from how we designed our rooms to how we trained our employees—had to serve this long-term vision.

Attracting the Right Guests, Not Just Any Guests

Instead of trying to cater to all travelers, I focused on one clear segment:

- Cultural Explorers—Travelers who sought authentic, meaningful experiences over typical tourist stays.
- Solo Travelers and Digital Nomads—Guests who valued community, comfort, and personal connection.
- Couples and Small Groups—People looking for intimate, cozy stays with a personal touch.

Once I defined my ideal guest, I reshaped everything about Mirabelle to appeal to them.

- Personalized Stays: Instead of generic rooms, guests received tailored recommendations based on their interests—food tours, local art walks, hidden gems.

- Community Spaces: We designed cozy lounge areas, communal breakfasts, and storytelling evenings to help travelers connect.

- Locally Curated Experiences: We partnered with local artists, chefs, and guides to offer guests unique city adventures they couldn't find anywhere else.

The result? People didn't just stay at Mirabelle—they experienced it. And they told their friends.

Turning Guests into Advocates

One evening, a guest named Emily checked in—a solo traveler, visiting the city for the first time. Instead of just handing her a room key, we welcomed her with a handwritten city guide, filled with personal recommendations from our hospitality team.

The next morning, she told me, "This is the first time a hotel has ever made me feel truly at home."

Emily later shared her experience on social media, travel blogs, and by word of mouth. Soon, Mirabelle became a destination in itself—not because of traditional marketing, but because of the stories guests carried with them. That's when I realized the most powerful marketing isn't advertising—it's creating an experience people can't stop talking about.

Long-Term Success: From Vision to Target Image

A vision is more than a statement—it needs a target image to provide a clearer picture of the future. My target image for Mirabelle was a second boutique location—not a chain, but a carefully curated expansion, a loyal community of travelers who return year after year, feeling like family, and a training program for hospitality professionals, teaching them how to craft warm, unforgettable experiences.

But even as I dreamed big, I understood one thing: The future is unpredictable. No vision should be set in stone. To ensure long-term success, I had to continuously evaluate and refine our target image.

A vision should inspire—but it must also evolve.

The Pursuit of Excellence: A Moving Target

Excellence isn't a destination—it's a mindset. Even as Mirabelle flourished, I knew there would always be new challenges, there would always be ways to improve, and the pursuit of excellence never truly ends.

The most successful organizations don't settle—they continue to learn, adapt, and strive for more.

Why? Because the market doesn't wait for anyone. Innovation happens overnight. Customer expectations shift constantly. Competitors improve and evolve.

While some businesses focus on short-term wins, Mirabelle's long-term vision gave us stability, direction, and a reason to keep pushing forward. As I stood on the rooftop of Mirabelle one evening, I looked out at the city skyline. The warm glow of streetlights flickered below, the hum of life carrying through the air. Mirabelle was finally thriving. But what about the future?

I closed my eyes and imagined Mirabelle 10 years from now. It had new locations, carefully curated to maintain the boutique experience; a hospitality training program, ensuring that the spirit of Mirabelle lives on; and a global reputation, not for being the biggest, but for being the most beloved.

I smiled. Success wasn't just about what we had built; it was about where we were going.

Final Lesson: Attract the Right People, and They'll Attract More

Mirabelle didn't succeed by trying to appeal to everyone. We succeeded by:

- Identifying the guests who would love what we offered.
- Creating an experience designed just for them.
- Turning guests into passionate advocates who spread the word.

By following the KAIZUNO method, I found direction, and I also found that when you build something genuinely meaningful, the right people will find you, love you, and bring others along for the journey.

A strong vision isn't just a dream—it's the foundation for every decision. And when your vision is compelling enough, it won't just drive you forward. It will inspire everyone around you to come along for the ride.

Chapter Two

Thrive Through Relationships (STEP 2)

Success grows when you address the most pressing challenges of your interest groups. To do this, you need a deep understanding of their needs and expectations. When you show genuine interest in their concerns, you create solutions that inspire and build long-lasting, authentic relationships with your interest groups. By anticipating future demands and addressing potential conflicts with partners early on, you foster trust and create a strong foundation for sustainable success.

Involve Success-Relevant Interest Groups

Interest groups are groups of people and institutions that have an interest in your organization—and they are crucial to your success. You are part of it yourself. No matter which plan you pursue, you will only be successful if you try to satisfy the interest groups relevant to your success. Of course, you first need to know which specific interest groups are important and critical for your success.

In everyday life, you are surrounded by interest groups that have expectations and a specific interest in you. Some of these interest groups can be your parents, children, relatives, neighbors, friends, governmental organizations (e.g., tax authorities), and the environment around your family (e.g., waste management regulations of the local city administration).

You know the interest groups in your private life, you know their importance for you, you understand (at least some of) their needs and expectations and you have experience in responding to them. Now, you just apply that knowledge to your organizational context.

What Are Interest Groups and Why Are They So Important?

We use "interest group" in this book; a synonym would be "stakeholder". No matter which target you pursue, you will only be successful if you satisfy the interest groups critical for your success. The five typical interest groups of organizations are:

Customers

They are the recipients of your products and services. They expect more benefits from you than from your competitors; otherwise, they would buy from them. It is therefore important to know your customers' needs and expectations precisely, review them regularly, and respond to them better than your competitors.

Employees

These are all the people in your organization, from top management to temporary workers. If you know and understand the current expectations of your employees, you will be able to respond to them in an appropriate manner. This enables you to retain and attract the best people. The needs and expectations of your employees are quite individual and diverse. We use "employees" in this book and avoid "staff", since employees are valued members of the organization.

Partners and Suppliers

Every organization needs to cooperate with partners and suppliers to inspire customers with attractive products and services. While partners are typically organizations that work closely with you to be successful, suppliers serve your supply chain. Since customers only see your products and services, you bear full responsibility for your partners and suppliers, against your customers.

Society

Successful organizations know that they need to provide more than just first-class products and services for their customers. They understand that they also serve society at large and support any relevant sustainability requirements in order to be successful in the long term.

Generally, society includes all relevant interest groups that represent the global community, which has committed to the "17 Sustainability Development Goals (SDG)" for a better future with the 2030 Agenda under the umbrella of the United Nations. The guiding principle is to enable people around the world to live in dignity while at the same time preserve the natural foundations of life in the long term. This includes Economic, Social and Governance (ESG) aspects.

Key Decision-Makers

These are individuals and institutions that set the course for your organization. While it is possible to actively influence the expectations of key decision-makers within your own organization—e.g., your directors or your board—you are merely the recipient of expectations from many other external key decision-makers—e.g., investors, shareholders, regulatory bodies, government agencies or media, and public opinion.

To understand all those influences on your organization better, and their complex interactions, you can create a graphic version of your organization's **ecosystem** as a simple yet powerful picture. Imagine your organization in the middle and four circles around it. Your internal interest groups (employees and internal key decision-makers) sit on the innermost circle. The next circle could include your most important external interest groups, e.g., your key customers, partners and your most influential decision-makers, and important society-related bodies.

Less important customers, suppliers, and less influential external decision-makers could sit on the third circle, while the outermost 4th circle could be reserved for the wider society, relevant megatrends, and other global influences. You could even put your key competitors somewhere in your ecosystem, as their activities can fundamentally influence the success of your organization.

Which Interest Groups Are Most Relevant?

If you want to bring a highly innovative product onto the market that is ahead of its time, then your customers with an affinity for technology are relevant to you first.

If you want to use the "Internet of Things" (IoT) in your organization, you need employees who have the necessary know-how.

If you need reliable amounts of sustainable energy, reliable energy suppliers with knowledge and experience in renewable energy are relevant for you.

If you want to strengthen your organization's resilience to mental illness, a certain part of society is relevant for you, e.g., psychologists and family members.

If you want to export to the EU, the requirements of the EU Commission in Brussels are relevant for you as an important decision-maker.

By taking key interest groups into account before you draft your plan toward a successful future, you reduce the risk of mistakes and wrong decisions, thereby increasing the chances for success.

How to Prioritize Relationships with Interest Groups

Managing relations with interest groups properly is one of the most important tasks of any organization, since no organization can exist without interest groups. This is just like in private life: nobody can exist without family, friends, partners, and society.

Organizations and interest groups interact every day, all the time. This is why it makes sense to manage relations with interest groups in structured ways, and to dedicate enough time and resources to these activities. As you know from your private life, proactive management of relations with interest groups can help you make the right decisions. Successful organizations know that appropriate management of interest groups is one of their most important tasks.

It is comparatively simple for leaders to manage relationships with employees, teams, and those key decision-makers who are inside the organization. It is much more challenging to manage valuable relationships with external interest groups such as customers, partners, and external key decision-makers. And it is even more difficult to manage relationships with those individuals, bodies, or rules and regulations who represent society and environment, since typically, you cannot interact with them directly.

In order to optimize your resources for relationship management with your interest groups, it may make sense to prioritize your relationship activities.

High Influence, High Interest: Actively engage and collaborate with these interest groups. Keep them informed and involved in your decision-making processes. Regularly consult them for feedback, as their support is crucial for your success.

High Influence, Low Interest: Keep these interest groups satisfied without overwhelming them with unnecessary details. They have significant power, so ensure that they remain supportive or neutral toward your organization.

Low Influence, High Interest: Keep these interest groups informed and show them that their concerns and interests are valued. While they may not have much power, they can still impact your organization's reputation and public perception.

Low Influence, Low Interest: Monitor these interest groups but avoid dedicating significant resources to actively engage them. Keep them informed at a basic level, ensuring that your organization is transparent but without overcommunicating. You know from your private life that different interest groups have different needs and expectations. You may even be familiar with the saying: "two people, three opinions".

If you use the 5 STEPS of KAIZUNO, you will build your plan upon the consolidated picture created from the various needs and expectations of your key interest groups. In other words, your plan will be an intelligent response to the needs and expectations from your interest groups.

What Are Typical Expectations of Interest Groups?

Customers may expect high-quality products and exceptional service, reliable deliveries, competitive prices, excellent collaboration, and seamless communication.

People may seek good leadership, fair appreciation, safe and supportive work environments, career development opportunities, and fair compensation.

Partners and suppliers may be interested in long-term, trustful and reliable collaboration, mutual benefit, and timely payments.

Society may require good citizenship, employment opportunities, sustainable energy solutions, or circular economy principles in production.

Key Decision-Makers may expect your organization to properly implement their decisions, investors expect financial returns, and sustainable growth.

While it is relatively easy to understand expectations, e.g., by asking interest groups (if they are approachable), it may be difficult to find out what their underlying needs are.

What Are Expectations and What Are Needs?

Expectations and needs are two concepts that are used in interactions and relationships in private and business context.

Expectations are statements about what is expected from a person or group. This can include a specific behavior, performance, or outcome. Expectations can originate from previous experiences, common practices, or established rules or agreements.

Needs, on the other hand, refer to what a person really requires to be happy, satisfied, and healthy. This can include physiological needs such as eating, drinking, and sleeping, but also psychological needs such as recognition, appreciation, and love. Needs are more profound and fundamental than expectations and are at the core of human motivation.

Five important differences between expectations and needs are:

- Origin: Expectations can be imposed by other people, society or culture, while needs come from within and originate from individuals themselves.
- Nature: Expectations are external and relate to what is expected of a person, while needs are internal and relate to what a person requires.
- Flexibility: Expectations can change and can be adjusted, while needs are fundamental and stable.

- Priority: Expectations typically have a lower priority than needs and can sometimes be ignored or changed when they conflict with needs.

- Impact on well-being: Fulfilled needs lead to greater well-being and happiness than fulfilled expectations, as they form the basis for well-being.

Example: Going to the hairdresser is often associated with the expectation of getting a suitable haircut with good value for money. The underlying need is "to feel good" or "to be more attractive". Many people value that a new hairstyle is recognized and appreciated by their social circle. To avoid risks or disappointments, many people therefore regularly visit their trusted hair salon. They prefer a service provider who knows their needs and whom they trust.

It is therefore important to know all expectations and at least some important needs of your interest groups, as they provide valuable indications for a promising relationship. Finally, here are examples that might help you identify the (hidden) needs behind (openly expressed) expectations:

Expectation: "I want you to be home by 10pm at the latest."

> Need: "I love you, so I don't want anything to happen to you, and I don't want to worry myself either."

Expectation: "I want you to check this invoice with accounting."

> Need: "I don't want to damage our image with a wrong invoice."

Expectation: "I want us to practice this presentation before the event."

> Need: "I want to look good in front of our customers and not embarrass myself."

Good relationships with interest groups, based on mutual trust over a long time, help to understand underlying needs beyond expectations. Good relationships also reduce the risk of misunderstanding.

Fully understanding the whole world of expectations—and also many of their underlying needs—of all relevant interest groups is an **excellent basis for your balanced plan** that will lead your organization toward success.

Understand the Expectations of Customers

Customers are the recipients of your products and services. They expect more benefit from you than from your competitions. It is therefore important to know exactly what benefits your customers expect and to review them regularly.

"The customer who goes to the DIY store and wants to buy a drill often only needs a hole in the wall."

—Peter Drucker

Who Are the Customers and What Do They Expect?

It may sound unbelievable, but in many organizations, there is a lack of clarity about who exactly "the customers" are. The authors of this book have observed or moderated many discussions in different organizations evolving around the simple question: "Who is your customer?"

Take an elementary school. Typically, the first response you get—if you start discussing this question with teachers and parents—is: "Our customers are the pupils, since they are the beneficiaries of our teaching and education services." A second question of the moderator: "And why do you think your community/country spends so much money for the education of children?" typically delivers a second response that children are educated to acquire the knowledge needed to get a job, which will support their life and maybe their family as well. Some will add that the final beneficiaries of education services are employers (who earn money with that knowledge), and eventually the society (who gets taxes from employers). The key learning from this simple example is: the definition of "customer" depends on the **context**.

The next example shows that the definition of "customer" also depends on the **perspective**.

Take a car factory. The factory makes cars, factory sells them to dealers, who sell them to end-users, who drive them. Who is the customer?

Is it the person who buys and drives the car?

Is it the car dealer who buys the car in stock?

Is it the factory sales?

Is it the factory department who performs the final quality check at the end of the production line?

The best possible answer is: "All of them are customers." The quality department is the customer of production. Factory sales is the customer of the factory. The car dealer is the customer of factory sales. The driver is the customer of the car dealer.

If you buy a car and something goes wrong, what do you do? You contact your dealer, since this is the last link in the customer chain. If the problem cannot be solved by the dealer, he contacts factory sales, and if the problem is production issue, the factory finally improves production processes to rule out the possibility of the problem occurring again.

Alternatively, from a factory sales perspective, dealers could be classified as partners and drivers as customers. The factory engineer who conducts the final quality check of a new car is an employee of the factory, but in his role, this person represents the first customer level for the factory.

We encourage you to have these discussions in your organization about your interest groups, before you start to understand their expectations and explore their underlying needs. If the role of interest groups is not clear or is misunderstood, there is a risk that expectations will be misinterpreted.

This could lead to an inadequate plan, which could have a negative impact on your success.

> *"No customer ever buys a product. He always buys what the product does for him."*
>
> —Peter Drucker

What Do Customers Expect and What Do They Need?

Only if you know the current expectations and needs of your customers, you can inspire and satisfy them with your products and services. Here are some typical expectations from customers, and associated underlying needs:

Product and Service Quality

Customers expect the products and services that they buy to be of high quality and to meet their requirements. Related needs could include reliability, trust, reputation, status.

Customer Service

Customers expect excellent service, including quick responses to inquiries and effective solutions to their problems. Related needs could include respect, reliability, convenience.

Value for Money

Customers expect the cost of a product or service to be in proportion to the quality and benefits they derive from it. Related needs could include fairness, justification, trust.

Transparency and Honesty

Customers expect organizations to be transparent and honest in their communication and business practices. Related needs could include trust and credibility, informed decision-making, fairness, and respect.

Sustainability and Ethical Behavior

More and more customers expect companies to act sustainably and ethically responsible, including respect of human rights and minimizing their environmental footprint. Related needs could include responsibility, integrity, future security.

Instead of products and services, customers increasingly expect solutions to their problems and responses to their needs.

Understand the Expectations of Employees

Employees are all people in your organization with an employment contract, from management to temporary workers. Highly motivated employees perform very well and inspire customers with very good products and services.

"Don't just give people what they expect, but what they deserve."

—Warren Buffet, Investor

What Do Employees Expect and What Do They Need?

If you know the current expectations and needs of your employees, you can successfully attract and retain your best talents. Here are some typical expectations from employees, and associated underlying needs:

Fair Pay

Employees expect fair pay and benefits commensurate with their tasks and performance, experience and market norms. Related needs could include: financial security, recognition, fairness, motivation, stability and job security.

Good and Safe Working Conditions

Employees expect a safe and healthy working environment that promotes their physical and mental health. Related needs could include: physical well-being and health, trust that leaders care, recognition, motivation.

Good Corporate Culture

Employees expect a corporate culture that promotes respect, diversity and appreciation, in which they feel comfortable and valued. Related needs could include: dignity, psychological safety and mental well-being, equity, sense of belonging and inclusion, collaboration and team work, social connection.

Training and Development Opportunities

Employees expect opportunities for professional development and training to improve their skills and advance their careers. Related needs could include: trust in leadership, job satisfaction, appreciation and recognition, autonomy, confidence, engagement and motivation.

Valuation of Daily Work

They expect their work to be seen and valued and their contributions to be recognized. Related needs could include: Appreciation, adequate work-life balance, open communication, fun and enjoyment.

In addition to these expectations that employees have of their employer, employees also have expectations of other employees, their colleagues. Here is an example of a detective organization which employs criminal investigators. Employees expect from their colleagues:

Professional Behavior

They expect their colleagues to act professionally at all times, both internally and in public, by respecting the dignity and rights of all persons with whom they come into contact in their work.

Thorough Investigations

They expect their colleagues to be meticulous, careful and conscientious in their investigations to ensure that all relevant evidence is collected and properly documented.

Compliance with Laws and Procedures

They expect their colleagues to comply with all relevant laws, regulations and internal procedures to ensure the integrity of their investigations.

Effective Communication

They expect their colleagues to be able to communicate clearly and effectively, both verbally and in writing, in order to convey information accurately and comprehensibly.

Teamwork and Collaboration

They expect their colleagues to work together effectively and share information to solve complex cases.

Understand the Expectations of Partners and Suppliers

Every organization needs cooperation in order to inspire customers with attractive products and services. Partners are usually organizations that cooperate on an equal footing and pursue long-term goals. Suppliers, however, supply goods and services.

Since customers see only your performance, you bear full responsibility for your partners and suppliers. The better you perform as an organization in your area or business, the more attractive you are for the best partners and suppliers. Dealing responsibly with sustainability issues is becoming increasingly important for an organization's attractiveness for the best partners and suppliers.

How Do Organizations Work Together with Partners and Suppliers?

You can strengthen your competitiveness, promote growth, and increase success through smart selection, appreciative cooperation, and responsible management of your partners and suppliers.

Good organizations work together with partners, e.g., to develop new products and services or form alliances that benefit both sides. This mutual benefit is the key characteristics of successful and sustainable partnerships. Good organizations work closely together with partners on a long-term basis to achieve common goals, which can lead to exciting innovations and new business models. Partners are generally important in order to achieve success goals.

Suppliers are typically part of the supply chain and supply raw materials, components, parts or finished products, and services. Since suppliers also buy from other suppliers, supply chains are structured in "tiers": your first-tier suppliers deliver their products and services directly you, while second tier suppliers provide their goods and services to first-tier suppliers. In Europe, the social responsibility of larger organizations, e.g., regarding environmental regulations, extends beyond the first tier of suppliers into lower tiers.

In order to fulfill their responsibility toward suppliers, responsible organizations use audits and assessments, and support their suppliers in making improvements.

What Do Partners and Suppliers Expect and What Do They Need?

Only if you know the current expectations and (at least some) needs of your partners and suppliers, you can successfully cooperate and work with them. Key to success is mutual benefit. Typical expectations from partners and suppliers, and associated needs are:

Compliance with Contracts:

Partners and suppliers expect contractual agreements and obligations to be honored. Related needs could include reliability, fairness, mutual benefit, legal security, risk mitigation.

Transparent and Clear Communication:

Partners and suppliers want good communication in order to be able to work efficiently with you. Related needs could include trust, predictability, reduced uncertainty.

Ethical Business Practices:

Partners and suppliers expect responsible action and behavior, including compliance with relevant labor and environmental standards. Related needs could include integrity, long-term stability, reputation, risk mitigation.

Fairness and Respect:

Partners and suppliers expect fair business conditions and appreciation of their contributions to your success. Related needs could include mutual benefit, reliability, recognition.

Long-Term Relationships:

Partners and suppliers are looking for stable, long-term relationships and support when challenges arise. Related needs could include fairness, collaboration, valued partnership.

Understand the Expectations of Society

Successful organizations need more than just first-class products, talented employees and strong partners. They must also understand the expectations and needs of society and take them seriously in order to be successful in the long term. Today, all organizations are expected to make positive contributions to society beyond their pure purpose.

In contrast to customers, employees and partners and suppliers, communication with representatives of society is considerably more difficult because there is often no clear contact person. Society includes many different aspects of life, local and global ones. Some of these aspects may be more, others less important for your organization.

The most general description of society and related expectations are the United Nations' "17 Sustainable Development Goals (SDG)". The global community committed to these goals on September 25, 2015, during the United Nations Sustainable Development Summit held at the UN headquarters in New York, USA. These goals were adopted as part of the 2030 Agenda for Sustainable Development, a framework aimed at addressing global challenges such as poverty, inequality, climate change, and environmental sustainability. The agreement was signed by all 193 UN member states and officially came into effect on January 1, 2016. The guiding principle is to enable people around the world to live in dignity while at the same time preserve the natural foundations of life in the long term.

The 17 SDGs can be segmented into 3 key areas: Environmental (E), Social (S), and Governance (G). ESG is used as a framework of expectations related to corporate responsibility and sustainability.

As a responsible organization, you can analyze all ESG-related expectations and define the relevance in the context of your organization, since some ESG aspects may be more relevant for you than others. The result could be a shortlist of the global society's expectations of your organization.

Beyond those global expectations, you may need to consider other society-related expectations at local, regional, and national levels (e.g., from local councils, politicians, governments, or environmental organizations).

"It takes 20 years to build a good reputation and 5 minutes to destroy it. If you are aware of this, you approach things differently."

—Warren Buffet, Investor

While this enormous variety of expectations from society will probably surprise and overwhelm you, it is important to know that dealing responsibly with these expectations can be crucial not only for your success, but also for the reputation and even the existence of your organization.

Here are some examples of organizations that have suffered serious damage by not fulfilling their responsibility to society.

Volkswagen: The 2015 emissions scandal, where Volkswagen was found to have manipulated emissions data ("dieselgate"), resulted in substantial financial penalties and a tarnished reputation. Shareholders lost more than $40 billion in two months. Volkswagen had to pay tens of billions in damages and fines to customers and dealers. Some of the lawsuits are still ongoing.

A *global sportswear and lifestyle brand* faced significant allegations in the early 2000s regarding the use of child labor in its supply chain. Reports indicated that factories in countries like Indonesia employed workers as young as 15 and subjected them to excessive working hours. These revelations led to public outcry and scrutiny of labor practices, had an immediate negative impact on the stock price, and caused damage to the organization's reputation.

Grenfell Tower Fire: The 2017 Grenfell Tower fire in London, which resulted in a large number of fatalities, brought to light unethical practices by key suppliers. Investigations revealed that these companies had knowingly supplied highly flammable cladding materials and manipulated safety test results. The scandal led to severe reputational damage and legal scrutiny for the suppliers involved.

The final example highlights the responsibility of organizations for their suppliers.

Understand the Expectations of Key Decision-Makers

Key decision-makers are people and institutions that make important decisions for your organization. You can often actively influence the expectations of decision-makers within your own organization, e.g., board members, directors, or owners. If you are able to regularly meet them in person, you have direct access to their expectations. Typically, internal key decision-makers share their expectations not only verbally, but also in clearly formulated objectives and other written expectations.

With external key decision-makers, such as regulatory interest groups, local or global governments or shareholders, you are usually just the recipient of expectations, with the exception of limited influencing opportunities, e.g., via lobbying.

"Laws were made so that people are secure in their freedom."

—Marcus Tullius Cicero

Who Are Regulatory Interest Groups and What Do They Expect?

While external key decision-makers can have a variety of roles, regulatory interest groups are probably the largest group. Expectations of this interest group can include:

Regulatory compliance:

They expect organizations to comply with all applicable laws and regulations. This may include tax laws, environmental regulations, data protection laws, and labor laws.

Transparency:

They often expect organizations to be transparent in their management, finances, and business practices. This may include the disclosure of financial and operational information as well as information on their social and environmental impact.

Responsibility toward society:

They may expect organizations to an increasing extent to act ethically and responsibly toward society. This may include respecting human rights standards, avoiding corruption and bribery, and taking responsibility for the impact of their business practices on communities and a sustainable world.

Risk management:

They may expect organizations to implement appropriate and effective risk management practices to prevent and mitigate potential risks to their operations, local and global society. This may include the establishment of risk assessments, risk prevention measures, emergency and crisis management and business continuity management.

Many of those expectations are clearly communicated, e.g., by laws or compliance regulations. However, these expectations can change, sometimes rapidly and without much warning—maybe as a result of political or economic changes, or global disruptions (e.g., COVID-19).

Because many external key decision-makers may have a decisive influence on the success of your organization, it is therefore very important to anticipate critical expectations of this interest group.

"The best way to predict the future is to create it."

—Peter Drucker (often attributed to Abraham Lincoln)

Foresee Probable Future Expectations

Unfortunately, it is not enough to understand the current expectations of your interest groups. If you want to act proactively in fast-changing times, you need to anticipate future expectations.

The major advantage of understanding future expectations will become fully clear in the next STEP. You will develop your plan mainly on the basis of expectations from your interest groups. Your plan will be much more focused on the future if it includes (potential) expectations of your interest groups. This will further reduce your high-level risks, or in other words, your plan will deliver your success with a much higher probability.

To find out about future expectations of interest groups, you need suitable predictive, simulation, or research instruments. Here are some proven examples of additional approaches that may also work for you:

- Observation of (innovative) market leaders
- Observation of competitors
- Observation of megatrends
- Observation of technology trends
- Review of relevant draft legislation
- Developments in patents
- Valuations of startups

In addition, professional risk management tools can provide you with valuable information on probable risks and effective preventive measures. We will explain later that the establishment of an "early warning system" can be a highly effective approach to master this challenge.

Ways to Understand Expectations of Interest Groups

Understanding individual expectations of all relevant interest groups is critical to address their individual needs effectively, which fosters strong relationships. There are many ways to gather expectations. It is a challenging leadership task to identify those methods and approaches that fit to the specific nature of relationships in the best possible way.

Due to the different nature of relationships, there is no standard way to gather expectations from interest groups. Rather, approaches and instruments need to be adapted to match the relationship requirements of specific interest groups. What may work for customers might not work for people or key decision-makers. Ways that work for large organizations may not work for small- or medium-size companies. Some methods are culture-specific. Some work better in a digital version, others might not.

As organizations develop, the portfolio of ways and instruments to collect expectations from interest groups has to be adapted. In any case, the ways to collect interest group expectations have to be optimized to match the preferences of interest groups regarding communication.

While we discuss ways to gather expectations of interest groups here, we will also cover ways to collect perception feedback of the same interest groups later. In both cases, the organization communicates with the same interest group, but the purpose of those two interactions is fundamentally different.

You gather expectations before you draft your plan (as a response to these expectations) and before you implement it; e.g., to design and manufacture your products and services and deliver them to your customers.

You collect feedback after you have implemented your plan to find out how satisfied your customers are with your products and services. These insights will enable you to further improve your plan and processes.

Before we talk about collecting feedback in STEP 5, let's focus now on ways to understand expectations. What are the most common methods, approaches, and instruments for that purpose? In any case, you need to treat every interest group individually, sometimes even individual entities within the same interest group (e.g., larger and smaller suppliers, or representatives of different hierarchical levels).

The most common approach to collect expectations is personal dialogues between organizational leaders (acting as relationship managers) with representatives of interest groups. In suitable settings (e.g., at a nice place over dinner, not in offices), representatives of interest groups will feel inspired to talk openly about their expectations. Leaders may ask open questions and listen to what the representative has to say.

A variation of individual and personal dialogues could be focus group meetings with a small number of interest group representatives, which are facilitated by leaders (relationship managers) as interactive discussions. Sometimes, those focus groups generate a larger range of expectations. It works specifically well with employees at lower levels in organizations.

Dialogues and group meetings work well for customers, employees, partners and suppliers, some key decision-makers and some society representatives. For many key decision-makers and most society and environmental representatives, you need other approaches.

Think of members of a governance board or shareholders. Most of them cannot be contacted directly. Typically, they explain their expectations crystal-clear in written directions (e.g., boards) or share their expectations via various media (e.g., shareholders).

While members of the local society may be directly approachable, expectations from the wider society and important sustainability requirements are rather shared via laws, regulations, or specific media. The global framework for expectation of society are the ESG-structured 17 SDGs, as previously explained.

This is why your organization needs to define your specific, customized set of approaches and instruments to understand expectations from all your important interest groups. Benchmarking of instruments with other organizations can help as an inspiration, but can also be dangerous, e.g., if the nature of relationships with interest groups is different.

Think Twice Before You Substitute Human Interaction with Interest Groups by AI-Powered Bots

More and more organizations use digital tools to interact with their customers and other interest groups. With AI support, the aim is to appear modern and innovative; however, in most cases, the key driver is cost savings. Apart from the fact that AI bots today are far from perfect, they are fundamentally changing the way you interact with your interest groups. In most cases, the targeted interest groups are not asked for their consent beforehand, but are rather confronted with the new technology as a surprise.

There is at least a subliminal suspicion of the targeted interest group that the organization is using digital methods only to save costs (which is true, in most cases). This can cause anger, frustration and rejection, which could worsen relationships, damage trust, and ultimately affect the success of the organization that introduced these bots in the first place.

So, before you consider using digital technologies, e.g., to collect expectations from your interest groups, discuss this option openly with them before you implement your AI chatbot. Or you don't, for a reason.

"You can't just ask customers what they want and try to give it to them. By the time you've finished it, they want something else."

—Steve Jobs, Founder of Apple

Expectations Change Over Time!

Like in your private life, your ecosystem of interest groups is made of human beings, and human beings keep changing their minds all the time. If you have established trusted relationships with your interest groups, and you use these strong relationships to collect their expectations at regular intervals, you will probably detect changes early enough to act.

It is important to define those intervals at a frequency that fits to the dynamics of your interest groups. If your interest group trusts and respects you, they will alert you about their change of mind before you even ask. The best way to ensure you are always up-to-date with the latest expectations is an early warning system, which will be explained later.

Know How Competitors Influence Your Business

Most businesses typically consider customers, employees, partners and suppliers, society and decision-makers as their primary interest groups. However, competitors also hold a stake in your organization—though mostly with hostile intentions.

Their primary goal may be to outperform or limit the success of your organization. This is why understanding their plans and expectations can provide valuable competitive intelligence that can be used to increase the success of your own organization.

Competitors can impact your organization in multiple ways:

Market influence: by shaping industry standards, customer expectations, and pricing models that can negatively influence your success.

Innovation pressure: by driving the need for continuous improvement and differentiation. This can inspire or hurt you, depending on your response.

Regulatory impact: by lobbying efforts that can influence industry regulations against you.

Talent acquisition and retention: They compete for skilled employees, affecting workforce dynamics with negative effects for you.

This is why you should acknowledge your competitors as an additional external interest group, who can directly or indirectly affect your success. You can gain insight into their intentions, using the following approaches.

Competitive intelligence and market research: industry reports and benchmarking can reveal key competitor priorities, monitoring public communications often highlight strategic directions and customer reviews and feedback can reveal gaps or weaknesses to exploit.

Direct observations and reverse engineering: product and service comparisons can be used to refine your organization's own offerings, supply chain and partnership monitoring can provide insight into cost structures and operational efficiencies, and talent moves and hiring trends can reveal areas where your competitors are expanding or innovating.

Engaging with industry networks and events: trade shows and conferences can provide valuable informal intelligence, and competitor employee insights can provide perspectives on internal competitor plans.

Digital and social media monitoring: competitor keyword tactics and advertising spend can provide insights into marketing focus areas of competitors, and their social media engagement can help to uncover unmet market needs.

Once you understand your competitors' intentions, you can optimize your plan in several ways (STEP 3).

Differentiation and competitive advantage: addressing your competitor weaknesses can help identify problems that your competitors struggle with; this knowledge can be used to enhance customer acquisition. By ensuring that products and services stand out through innovation or superior customer service, your unique value proposition (UVP) can be enhanced.

Strategic positioning and pricing tactics: by anticipating market moves of your competitors, your own product launches and pricing can be adjusted to stay ahead in the market. Defensive plans and preparing countermeasures can help to protect market share against aggressive competitor moves.

Innovation and adaptation: learning from competitors' successes while avoiding their mistakes and investing in technology and talent can be used to securing key talent before competitors do.

Collaboration opportunities: in some cases, collaboration with competitors (e.g., shared supply chains, industry alliances) can drive mutual benefits.

Engaging in industry groups can help shape favorable regulations and technological standards, thereby providing competitive advantages.

Analyze the Overall Situation for Potential Risks

Imagine you have collected all relevant expectations from all interest groups that are critical for your success (including information about your competitors). It is in the nature of things that most of those expectations are diverse. Some fit together, while others contradict or even exclude each other.

In STEP 3, you will use expectations of your interest groups as the main input for your plan. Before you can do that, you have to conduct two checks:

1.   Identify and remove risky expectations.
2.   Resolve serious conflicts between expectations.

Let's first address risky expectations since they can be dangerous for you, as input for your plan.

What Are Risky Expectations, and How to Handle Them

Success-related risks, if they may be misaligned with your long-term goals.

Example: customers expect you to lower prices aggressively, but this could erode your profitability.

Operational risks, if they may disrupt your daily business processes.

Example: your employees expect full remote work, but certain critical operations strictly require on-site presence.

Financial risks, if they may impact your profitability or financial stability.

Example: your suppliers expect extended payment terms, while your financial health requires strict cash flow management.

Regulatory and compliance risks, if they could lead to legal or ethical violations.

Example: an interest group expects you to bypass certain ethical rules or regulations to speed up product launches.

Reputational Risks, if they could damage your brand image.

Example: interest groups expect you to neglect sustainability targets that may result in negative public perception and damage your reputation.

After identifying all risky expectations, you can classify them according to probability and impact, and compare the result with your risk acceptance threshold (more about risk management in STEP 3).

Then you can adjust all those expectations with a risk above threshold and bring the risk level down to an acceptable level. Example: Instead of lowering prices drastically, offer targeted discounts.

Please remember that good relations with your interest groups are fundamentally important for your sustained success. This is why you should never adjust expectations without communicating and discussing those adjustments with the interest groups concerned, to manage their expectations and to justify your decision.

As soon as you have removed risky expectations, you should solve serious conflicts between different expectations, as a last check before you start planning.

Resolve Serious Conflicts in the Overall Situation

Expectations of interest groups are not necessarily aligned. Rather, many expectations contradict each other. This happens in any organization, since it is a natural phenomenon that you also know from your private life.

Finding ways to balance contracting expectations in the best possible way, without alienating interest groups, is a very challenging leadership task. The importance of this task and its influence on success is completely underestimated by most organizations.

Potential conflicts of interest can exist between different interest groups, and sometimes there are even conflicting interests between different entities of one interest group, e.g., between different key decision-makers, different suppliers, or different social representatives.

If all potential conflicts are fully understood and solved properly, leaders can put together a coherent set of expectations, free of conflicts. This creates a robust and sound basis for your balanced plan.

If certain expectations do not fit into this consistent picture, leaders have to decide how to properly approach interest groups to discuss and manage their expectations. Every successful salesperson knows this challenge and has learned effective ways how to manage this.

"It is more difficult to shatter a preconceived opinion than an atom."

—Albert Einstein

Managing expectations of interest groups is a core leadership responsibility and cannot be delegated, neither to partners nor to consultants. Wrong decisions and incompetent management of interest group expectations can easily jeopardize the success of your organization.

While it is never possible to satisfy expectations of all interest groups all the time, this target could still be the "vision" of the leadership team.

Constantly and even proactively trying to ensure the best possible balance between conflicting expectations in a volatile environment is the most important prerequisite for sustained success. Here are some typical examples of conflicts between interest group expectations, and opportunities to balance them.

Shareholders vs. employees: shareholders typically prioritize financial returns, while employees are concerned with job security, fair wages and favorable working conditions. A balanced approach could be to invest in employee development, leading to higher efficiency, which ultimately benefits both employees and shareholders.

Customers vs. suppliers: customers demand high-quality products at competitive prices, while suppliers seek fair compensation for their goods and services. A balanced approach could be to communicate openly to find the best possible balance between cost and price; this can create a win-win scenario. Good organizations support their suppliers to reduce costs by innovation without compromising quality.

Investors vs. society: investors often prioritize short-term financial returns and may view society-related initiatives as a cost rather than an investment for the future. A balanced approach could be to demonstrate the long-term financial benefits of society-related initiatives to investors, such as competitive advantage on the market and enhanced attractiveness as employer.

Don't Miss Last-Minute Changes of Expectations

Collecting expectations from interest groups and consolidating them into a consistent set of expectations will take some time. So, it may happen that individual interest groups change their mind "last minute", just as you are about to finalize your expectation picture. If you don't take these changes into account, you use outdated expectations to craft your plan (in STEP 3). This means that your plan is outdated, and if you implement it, you may steer your organization into the wrong direction, which could affect your success.

To ensure that you are always aware of any changes in expectations in good time until "the last minute" (or even before they happen), you can introduce an effective *early warning system* for your ecosystem of interest groups.

Beyond common ways and instruments to "look into the future", which were explained earlier, a professional early warning system creates a framework of sensors in the interest group ecosystem. These sensors must be individually adapted to the respective interest groups in order to be effective. Examples could be as follows:

Customers: Social media monitoring of customer conversations, dissatisfaction or trends in complaints. Analysis of product use patterns or service metrics to detect early signals of declining engagement or emerging needs. Leveraging employees, partners, or suppliers who are closest to customers as informal sensors.

People: Conducting regular short surveys to monitor job satisfaction, workplace culture, and expectations. Structured exit interviews to identify common reasons for dissatisfaction or departure. Analyses of themes in feedback channels like town halls, online discussions, or people and talent platforms.

Partners and suppliers: Real-time tracking of key supplier metrics like delivery timelines, quality, and compliance. Alerts for delays in raw material shipments can highlight potential supply chain disruptions. Subscribing to industry-specific newsletters or feeds for insights on market or regulatory changes potentially affecting your suppliers.

Society: Use of smart online tools to monitor how your organization is perceived in the news and by social activists. Creating direct channels to gather community input on societal concerns. Partnerships with or monitoring of NGOs relevant to your industry to understand shifts in societal expectations.

Key decision-makers: Subscribing to newsletters, updates and notifications from relevant regulatory agencies to track upcoming policy changes. Engaging with sector specific bodies or trade associations that provide early insights into regulatory trends. Using online tools to monitor legislative developments and regulatory announcements. Maintaining open communication channels with regulators.

Competitors: Using smart tools to track competitors' strategies and market shifts. Tracking competitors' patents or R&D efforts to anticipate new technologies. Attending events to gather insights on competitors' positioning and innovations. Asking customers to provide comparative feedback about other suppliers, who are your competitors.

The best early warning systems can identify change signals in your ecosystem in real time and even in a predictive way, if AI-powered data analytics and simulation models are used.

As soon as any sensor signal flashes, you can adapt the balance of expectations accordingly and quickly, if your STEP 2 activities are flexible and agile. If you do that adaptation faster than your competitor, you create a substantial competitive advantage.

No Business Succeeds in Isolation

Customers, employees, suppliers, and partners all contribute to long-term success. KAIZUNO emphasizes the importance of understanding and managing expectations of interest groups to build trust and create strong foundations for sustainable growth.

Maya Dani quickly learned that success wasn't just about her ideas—it was about how well she connected with the people who made her business possible.

Thrive Through Relationships (STEP 2) - Application

Involve Success-Related Interest Groups

One of the most important lessons I learned in building Mirabelle was this: Success isn't achieved alone. It is built with the right people.

At first, I believed that as long as I had a clear vision and a strong work ethic, my hotel would thrive. But I quickly realized that no matter how passionate I was, I couldn't do it all on my own. To turn Mirabelle into a long-term success, I had to involve the right interest groups—people and organizations who had a stake in our growth.

Identifying the Key Interest Groups

I asked myself:

- Who directly influences the success of my hotel?
- Who benefits from Mirabelle thriving?
- Whose support will make a real difference?

The answer was clear:

Customers—The people who would decide if we were worth coming back to (or not).

Employees—The heart of the hotel, shaping the experience every single day.

Partners and Suppliers—The people providing the ingredients, furniture, and services that defined our quality.

Key Decision-Makers—Those who helped finance the dream and expected a return on their trust.

Society—The people who could either support or reject our presence in their neighborhood.

Each of these interest groups had expectations, needs, and concerns—and if I ignored them, Mirabelle wouldn't last.

Prioritizing Relationships: Who Matters Most?

One of the first things I learned was that not all interest groups have the same level of influence. To focus our efforts effectively, we used the Influence-Interest Matrix, which helped us classify our interest groups into four categories:

Engage Actively—High influence, high interest. These are the people who shape our business daily—returning customers, senior employees, key partners, and investors. We made sure to engage with them directly and often.

How we applied this at Mirabelle: We set up personal concierge services for VIP guests, employee listening sessions to improve operations, and regular check-ins with investors and regulators.

Keep Satisfied—High influence, low interest. These are powerful groups that don't interact often but can impact our future, like local authorities and occasional corporate clients. We ensured that they stayed informed and content.

How we applied this at Mirabelle: We set up quarterly updates for regulatory bodies, special incentives for corporate travel planners, and an efficient supplier management system to maintain good relationships.

Keep Informed—Low influence, high interest. These people love our brand but don't have decision-making power—such as casual visitors, prospective employees, and small vendors. We kept them engaged through brand storytelling and clear communication.

How we applied this at Mirabelle: We started social media engagement with travel bloggers and first-time guests, career newsletters to keep potential employees interested, and supplier networking events to encourage long-term partnerships.

Low—Low influence, low interest. These are people who care about our brand but don't have direct decision-making power. They might not drive immediate business outcomes, but their loyalty and enthusiasm make them valuable advocates. Keeping them engaged through storytelling and transparent communication helped strengthen their connection with Mirabelle.

How we applied this at Mirabelle: We engaged travelers and first-time guests on social media and email newsletters to keep them excited about our brand. We sent prospective employees career updates and company culture insights to maintain their interest in future roles, and for small vendors and potential partners, we hosted networking events and shared industry insights to encourage collaboration. For local community members, we kept them informed about Mirabelle's sustainability and charity initiatives to build goodwill. By prioritizing high-influence, high-interest interest groups first, we ensured that we focused on the relationships that would have the greatest impact.

Turning Interest Groups into Partners

Understanding who mattered was one thing. Making them feel valued and included was another. I had to be intentional in the process.

Customers: I didn't just treat guests as customers; I treated them as co-creators of the experience. I actively sought their feedback, listened to their suggestions, and made real changes based on their needs.

Example: When guests mentioned they wanted more local experiences, I partnered with local guides and artisans to create exclusive tours and workshops.

Employees: Instead of just expecting my team to follow instructions, I empowered them to take ownership of their roles.

Example: One of my receptionists, Sofia, suggested a personalized welcome note system, which became one of our most loved guest experiences.

Partners and Suppliers: I didn't treat suppliers as mere vendors—I built relationships based on trust and shared success.

Example: When our local coffee supplier was struggling financially, we collaborated to create an exclusive Mirabelle coffee blend, giving them a steady income while providing our guests with a signature experience.

Key Decision-Makers: I kept them informed, transparent, and engaged in our journey—not just with financial reports, but with stories of real impact.

Example: Instead of just reporting revenue numbers, I shared guest testimonials, team success stories, and expansion plans that kept them invested emotionally, not just financially.

Society: I made sure Mirabelle didn't just exist in the city—it became part of the city.

Example: We hosted community events, collaborated with local businesses, and ensured that our success also meant success for the neighborhood around us.

By building strong, trust-based relationships with each of these groups, Mirabelle didn't just operate—it thrived as part of a larger ecosystem.

Beyond Expectations: Understanding Needs

At first, I thought understanding expectations was enough. But over time, I learned that expectations and needs are not the same thing.

Expectations—What people ask for.

Needs—The deeper, often unspoken, motivations behind their expectations.

For example:

Guest at front desk

> Expectation: "I need you to fix this billing error right away."
>
> Need: "I want to feel confident that I'm being treated fairly and that I can trust your service."

Guest to restaurant waiter

> Expectation: "Can you make sure my food comes out quickly?"
>
> Need: "I'd like to relax and enjoy my meal without feeling rushed or forgotten."

Guest to room housekeeping

> Expectation: "Please don't enter my room until after noon."
>
> Need: "I want a sense of privacy and control over my space while I'm staying here."

Understanding the hidden needs behind expectations helped me respond in ways that created true trust and loyalty. It wasn't enough to meet requests—I had to anticipate the deeper motivations driving them.

Final Lesson: Build a Circle of Success

I used to think that running a business meant standing alone as a leader. But I learned that true success comes when you bring people into your vision and make them feel like part of something bigger.

- Customers became our storytellers.
- Employees became our ambassadors.
- Partners and suppliers became our allies.
- Key decision-makers became our believers.
- Society became our biggest supporters.

That's how Mirabelle didn't just survive—it thrived, because when you invest in relationships, you invest in long-term success.

Understand the Expectations of Customers

One of the biggest mistakes I made early on at Mirabelle was assuming I knew exactly what my customers wanted. I thought that if I offered beautiful rooms, friendly service, and great amenities, guests would be satisfied. But I quickly learned that what I thought was important wasn't always what my guests actually valued. Many businesses confuse what customers say they want with what they truly need.

Here's the key difference:

Expectation: "I want a fast check-in process."

> Underlying Need: "I don't want to feel stressed after traveling."

Expectation: "I expect fresh, organic food."

Underlying Need: "I want to maintain my health and feel good."

Expectation: "I expect loyalty program rewards."

Underlying Need: "I want to feel valued as a returning guest."

At Mirabelle, we didn't just listen to what guests asked for, we focused on the why behind their expectations. That's what allowed us to fulfill and even exceed their needs. Their expectations weren't just about a nice stay—they were about how the experience made them feel.

The Wake-Up Call: A Lesson in Listening

One afternoon, I received an online review from a guest that made me stop in my tracks. *The hotel is nice, but it feels like just another place to sleep. I wish there was more warmth, more attention to detail, and more effort to make guests feel special.* That hit me. I had been focusing on delivering a service— but what guests really wanted was a personal, emotional connection. That day, I made a decision. I was going to stop assuming and start listening.

Learning What Customers Really Expect

I started gathering real insights from guests using different approaches:

- Personal Conversations—I made it a habit to chat with guests during breakfast, at check-in, or in the lounge.
- Feedback Cards and Surveys—We added a quick, easy-to-fill form at checkout, asking guests what they loved and what could be better.
- Social Media and Reviews—I paid attention not just to ratings, but to the words guests used to describe their experience.

What I Discovered: The Hidden Expectations of Customers

As I started listening, I realized that guests' expectations went far beyond what I had assumed. They wanted:

More Personalization—Guests didn't want to feel like just another booking number; they wanted their stay to feel tailored to them.

A Sense of Belonging—Some solo travelers wanted privacy, others wanted spaces where they could meet people and feel part of a community.

Seamless, Stress-Free Service—Business travelers wanted everything to be effortless and intuitive—fast check-ins, good wi-fi, and quiet workspaces.

Local and Authentic Experiences—Many guests wanted more than just a place to sleep—they wanted to experience the city in a real, meaningful way.

Adapting Mirabelle to Meet Guest Expectations

Once I truly understood what guests wanted, I started making small but impactful changes. We personalized welcomes—guests received a handwritten welcome note and recommendations based on their interests; encouraged social gatherings for solo travelers. We introduced weekly coffee tastings and storytelling nights to help guests connect; we aimed for fast and easy service for business travelers. We optimized mobile check-ins, work-friendly lounge spaces, and late-night dining options. We created local experiences—we partnered with local artists, chefs, and guides to offer guests exclusive cultural experiences.

One guest, Emma, a solo traveler from Canada, told me: "This is the first time I have stayed at a hotel where I felt like I truly belonged. I didn't just visit the city—I became part of it." That's when I knew we were getting it right.

Who Are the Customers? A Crucial Question

Before you can fully understand customer expectations, you need to define who your customers really are. Many businesses struggle with this.

A hospital's patients are customers—but so are insurance companies.

A university's students are customers—but so are employers who hire graduates.

A hotel's guests are customers—but so are the travel agencies that send them.

Before defining customer expectations, a business must clearly define who their customers really are and focus on that customer's experience.

I learned from this insight that I have to treat every travel agency not just as a source of bookings, and not just as a business partner, but also as a valued customer. I wanted to earn their trust through consistency, transparency, and responsiveness. When they recommend my hotel, they put their reputation on the line—so I made it my mission to protect and elevate it.

Final Lesson: Customers Expect to Be Understood, Not Just Served

Understanding customers isn't about offering more—it's about offering what truly matters to them. A few takeaways:

- Listen before making assumptions.
- Identify what makes your customers feel valued.
- Make adjustments that enhance their experience—not just your business.

At Mirabelle, we don't just provide rooms. We provide experiences that feel personal, meaningful, and unforgettable. And that's why our guests don't just stay with us—they become part of our story.

Understand the Expectations of Employees

I remember the day one of my best employees, Aisha, a front desk manager, walked into my office looking nervous. "I love working here," she said, "but I am exhausted. I feel like I am always fixing problems, and sometimes I wonder if my work is really appreciated." That moment hit me. Aisha was one of my top performers. If she felt undervalued, how many others did too? It made me realize that employees don't just expect a pay check, they expect purpose, respect, and growth.

Without motivated and satisfied employees, a business can never succeed long term.

Understanding What Employees Really Expect

I started having open conversations with my team and quickly discovered what the employees valued most:

Fair Pay and Financial Security—Employees wanted to feel that their hard work was rewarded fairly and that they could rely on financial stability.

Safe and Supportive Work Environment—They expected physical and mental well-being to be a priority.

Recognition and Appreciation—Employees wanted to feel seen and valued for their contributions.

Clear Communication and Transparency—They expected honest conversations about decisions affecting them.

Career Growth and Development—They didn't just want a job, they wanted a future.

Work-Life Balance—They wanted flexibility and a healthy working environment.

A Sense of Purpose—They wanted to feel like their work mattered, that they were part of something bigger.

This wasn't about perks—it was about fundamental needs that directly impacted performance and retention.

The Turning Point: Adapting to Employee Expectations

Once I understood their needs, I started making intentional changes to create a workplace where employees felt motivated, supported, and valued.

Fair Pay and Financial Security: We reviewed salaries to ensure they were competitive and aligned with industry standards. We added performance-based bonuses to recognize outstanding work.

Safe and Supportive Work Environment: We improved break areas to make them more relaxing and stress-free. We created an open-door policy so employees felt safe speaking up about workplace concerns.

Recognition and Appreciation: We introduced a "Star of the Month" program to highlight outstanding contributions, and involved all employees in the appreciation process to ensure fairness and avoid envy. We started celebrating even small achievements with handwritten thank-you notes and public recognition.

Clear Communication and Transparency: I started holding monthly team meetings where employees could share concerns, ideas, and feedback—without fear. We introduced a company-wide chat channel where leadership openly shared updates and decisions.

Career Growth and Development: We implemented training programs so employees could learn new skills and advance in their careers. We offered mentorship opportunities to help team members grow professionally.

Work-Life Balance: We adjusted schedules to provide better flexibility for employees with families. We ensured that no one was overworked or felt pressured to work long hours.

Giving Employees a Sense of Purpose: We redefined roles so employees saw themselves not just as "staff" or "workers" but as talented storytellers, culture-builders, and the heart of Mirabelle.

The Transformation: How Employee Morale Shifted

After implementing these changes, I saw a huge shift in the way my team worked. Employees became more engaged, guest satisfaction improved because service was more authentic, and turnover rates dropped because people wanted to stay and grow with us.

One day, Aisha, the same employee who had once been on the verge of leaving, told me: "Maya, this is the first place I have worked where I actually feel valued. I don't just clock in and clock out—I feel like I'm part of something meaningful." That's when I knew we had done something right.

Employee Expectations Aren't Just About Leadership

While employees have **expectations of their employer**, they also have **expectations of each other**. For example**,** in **a hospital**, healthcare professionals expect their colleagues to:

Provide High-Quality Care—Ensure patients receive the best possible treatment and attention.

Follow Medical Protocols and Safety Standards—Adhere to hygiene, ethical guidelines, and hospital regulations.

Communicate Clearly and Accurately—Share critical patient information efficiently to prevent errors.

Support Each Other in High-Stress Situations—Work collaboratively during emergencies, surgeries, and complex treatments.

Respect Each Other's Roles and Expertise—Nurses, doctors, technicians, and administrators rely on each other's skills to function as a strong unit.

At Mirabelle, we reinforced teamwork and collaboration by encouraging cross-training, so employees could understand each other's roles; holding team-building activities, so employees built real connections; creating a culture of shared responsibility, so no one felt isolated in their work— because when employees respect each other, the entire organization thrives.

Final Lesson: A Thriving Business Starts with a Thriving Team

Understanding employee expectations isn't just about keeping them happy—it's about building a team that is passionate, motivated, and committed.

Employees want to feel appreciated. They need communication, respect, and a clear future.

If you take care of your team, they will take care of your guests.

At Mirabelle, we don't just hire employees—we invest in talented people who believe in our vision. And that's why our success is built not just on great service, but on great people.

Understand the Expectations of Partners and Suppliers

At Mirabelle, I quickly learned that success isn't just about guests and employees—it is also about the people behind the scenes. My suppliers and business partners were just as crucial to the hotel's long-term success as the team running it. But in the early days, I made a mistake—I treated suppliers like vendors, not partners. I would negotiate prices, place orders, and expect everything to work smoothly. Until one day, it didn't.

The Day the Breakfast Fell Apart

One morning, I walked into the kitchen, expecting the usual aroma of fresh pastries and coffee. Instead, I found chaos. Our local bakery supplier hadn't delivered the breakfast pastries, and our chef, Luis, was scrambling to find alternatives. I immediately called the bakery owner, Marco, frustrated. "What happened? You have never missed a delivery before."

There was a pause on the other end.

"Maya, we are struggling," Marco admitted. "Our costs have gone up, and we had to cut some deliveries. We didn't know how to tell you."

That hit me hard. I had been treating Marco as just a supplier, but to him, our partnership was personal. After that call, I realized I needed to rethink the way I worked with suppliers and business partners.

Instead of just focusing on what I needed, I started asking:

- What do my partners need to succeed?
- How can I ensure that our relationship is mutually beneficial?
- What are their long-term goals, and how can we grow together?

Here's what I discovered partners and suppliers expect:

Compliance with Contracts—They expect agreements and obligations to be honored.

Need: Reliability, fairness, mutual benefit, risk mitigation.

Transparent and Clear Communication—No one likes last-minute surprises or sudden changes. They want clear expectations and open conversations.

Need: Trust, predictability, reduced uncertainty.

Commitment and Stability—Many small suppliers depend on long-term partnerships, not just short-term contracts.

Need: Financial security, collaboration, trust.

Ethical Business Practices—Partners and suppliers expect responsible behavior, including compliance with labor and environmental standards.

Need: Integrity, long-term stability, reputation.

Fairness and Mutual Respect—Suppliers want to be treated as partners, not just service providers.

Need: Appreciation, reliability, recognition.

Long-Term Relationships—Partners and suppliers value stability and support when challenges arise.

Need: Consistency, shared growth, valued partnership.

If I wanted strong relationships with my partners and suppliers, I needed to invest in their success too.

Strengthening Supplier and Partner Relationships

After the breakfast delivery crisis, I changed how I worked with all my partners and suppliers.

I scheduled regular check-ins: Instead of only calling when I needed something, I started meeting with suppliers monthly to understand their challenges and needs.

I negotiated win-win contracts: Instead of just pushing for the lowest prices, I worked with suppliers to create agreements that worked for both of us.

I built backup supplier relationships: To avoid being caught off-guard again, I created secondary supplier partnerships—but still prioritized loyalty to my original vendors.

I supported local businesses: Instead of working with large corporate suppliers, I invested in local farms, bakeries, and artisans—helping them grow alongside Mirabelle.

One month after my talk with Marco, I received a message from him: "Maya, thank you. Because of your partnership, we are expanding and hiring two more bakers. We will never miss another delivery again." That's when I knew that Mirabelle wasn't just growing—we were helping others grow too.

Why a Partnership Mindset Matters

Many organizations treat suppliers like interchangeable vendors—focusing only on price and efficiency. But the best businesses know that partnerships drive long-term success. For example, in a technology company, software firms often rely on external IT service providers to help them develop, test, and launch new features.

If the relationship is purely transactional, issues arise: Developers work on short-term fixes instead of long-term innovation, security risks increase because of a lack of shared trust, and the company must constantly find new providers, disrupting workflows.

However, if the company builds true partnerships, external developers feel invested in the product's success, and security and compliance improve through close collaboration.

Innovation flourishes because teams work toward a shared goal.

At Mirabelle, I applied this same mindset to our supplier relationships. We stopped seeing them as vendors and started treating them as partners.

Final Lesson: Success Is Built Together

I used to think partners and suppliers existed to serve the business. Now, I know:

- True success happens when businesses support each other.
- Strong partnerships create reliability and trust.
- Fair treatment leads to long-term success, not just short-term gains.
- If you invest in your suppliers, they will invest in you.

At Mirabelle, we don't just have suppliers. We have partners who grow with us, succeed with us, and believe in our journey.

Understand the Expectations of Society

When I started Mirabelle, I was focused on two things: creating an incredible guest experience and running a successful business. But I soon realized that a hotel doesn't exist in isolation. It's part of a city, a community, and a larger social and environmental ecosystem. And if I ignored society's expectations, Mirabelle wouldn't just lose credibility—it could lose its place in the community.

The Turning Point: A Wake-Up Call About Sustainability

One morning, as I walked past the hotel's back entrance, I noticed something that unsettled me—our dumpsters were overflowing with plastic waste. Stacks of disposable coffee cups, food packaging, and single-use toiletry bottles were piled high, waiting to be taken away. At first, I ignored it— after all, waste management was just part of running a business. But then I overheard a conversation between two guests in the restaurant: "I love the hotel," one of them said, "but have you noticed how much plastic they use? I expected a place like this to be more sustainable."

That comment hit me like a brick. I had spent so much time perfecting the guest experience, yet I had overlooked something equally important—our impact on the environment.

I started asking myself:

- How much waste were we really generating every day?
- Were we making it easy for guests to make sustainable choices?
- Could we reduce our environmental footprint without compromising the guest experience?

That's when I realized: Society expects businesses to take real action on sustainability—not just talk about it.

Understanding What Society Expects from Businesses

I started paying attention to what mattered to the people around us, and here's what I learned:

Sustainability Matters: People expect businesses to operate ethically and responsibly—from reducing waste to sourcing locally.

Cultural Respect Is Key: A hotel shouldn't just exist in a city—it should embrace and celebrate its culture.

Job Creation and Fair Employment: Local communities want businesses that support fair wages and good working conditions.

Giving Back Is Valued: People respect companies that contribute to local causes and uplift communities.

Transparency Builds Trust: Customers, employees, and society at large expect businesses to be honest and accountable in their actions.

Once I understood these expectations, I shifted Mirabelle's focus—not just on profits, but on purpose.

Aligning Mirabelle with Society's Expectations

I wanted to ensure Mirabelle wasn't just a business—it needed to be a responsible, engaged member of society. We aligned our sustainability efforts with the United Nations' Sustainable Development Goals (SDGs):

SDG 12 (Responsible Consumption and Production)—Reducing waste and sourcing local ingredients.

SDG 8 (Decent Work and Economic Growth)—Creating fair wages and training programs for employees.

SDG 13 (Climate Action)—Implementing energy-efficient practices and reducing our carbon footprint.

This alignment ensured that our business was not just profitable, but also socially responsible.

How Mirabelle Became a Socially Responsible Business

We didn't just want to be in the city—we wanted to be part of the city.

We introduced:

Sustainability Initiatives: Zero-waste policies, energy-efficient systems, and eliminated single-use plastics.

Cultural Integration: We collaborated with local artists, musicians, and chefs to ensure Mirabelle truly reflected the spirit of the city.

Local Hiring and Fair Wages: We prioritized hiring local talent, paid fair wages, and created career development programs for our employees.

Community Support Programs: We started monthly initiatives, like hosting charity events and offering free hospitality training for young people.

The Impact: How Society Responded

One evening, a longtime guest, David, told me: "I used to travel without thinking about the impact my stay had. But when I see what Mirabelle is doing—supporting the city, the environment, and the people—I feel good about staying here."

That's when I knew being socially responsible wasn't just the right thing to do—it was something people valued and respected. And soon, we started attracting more conscious travelers, ethical investors, and employees who cared about making a difference.

Final Lesson: Business Is About More Than Profit—It's About Purpose

Society doesn't expect businesses to just make money—they expect them to make a difference. Sustainability isn't optional; it's expected. Respect for local culture isn't just nice—it's necessary. Giving back to the community strengthens your brand and your impact. A responsible business isn't only profitable, it's meaningful.

At Mirabelle, we don't just operate in a city; we exist to make it better.

Understand the Expectations of Key Decision-Makers

One thing I learned early on in my journey at Mirabelle is that every business, no matter how independent, is influenced by key decision-makers. These are the people and institutions that shape the business landscape.

Key decision-makers can include:

Investors and Financial Backers—The people funding or supporting the business.

Government and Regulatory Authorities—Those setting rules on operations, labor, safety, and sustainability.

Industry Leaders and Business Networks—Organizations that influence market trends and partnerships.

Local Community Leaders and Influencers—Figures who can either support or challenge a business's presence in a city.

If I ignored their expectations, I risked losing credibility, funding, or even the ability to operate.

The Investor Dilemma: A Lesson in Alignment

I remember the first time I had to negotiate with investors. Mirabelle was growing, and I needed financial backing to expand and renovate. I sat down with potential investors, eager to share my vision of a sustainable, experience-driven boutique hotel. But halfway through my pitch, one investor, Mr. Lindberg, interrupted me. "Maya, I love what you've built," he said, "but I think you're missing an opportunity. If you streamline the experience—cut the cultural elements, reduce local partnerships, and focus on high-margin international branding—you could scale much faster."

I felt my stomach drop. He was offering a path to rapid expansion, but at the cost of everything that made Mirabelle unique. That's when I realized: not all decision-makers share your vision—and not all opportunities are worth taking.

Understanding What Key Decision-Makers Expect

To make the right choices, I had to understand what different decision-makers expected and how to align their needs with my vision. Investors expect:

- A clear financial plan with stable revenue and growth potential.
- A scalable and sustainable model that ensures long-term success.
- Risk management strategies to protect their investment.

Regulators expect:

- Compliance with local, national, and international laws (labor, safety, environmental).
- Ethical business practices that meet transparency and accountability standards.

Industry leaders expect:

- Alignment with industry trends (e.g., digital innovation, sustainability).
- Strong collaborations and partnerships that elevate the business.

Community leaders expect:

- Respect for local traditions, economies, and cultural identity.
- Initiatives that contribute to job creation and social responsibility.

If I ignored these expectations, I wouldn't just be running a hotel—I'd be fighting uphill battles with powerful influencers.

Balancing Expectations Without Losing My Identity

With each of these groups, I had to negotiate and align expectations without sacrificing what made Mirabelle special.

For Investors: Instead of sacrificing authenticity for fast growth, I presented a sustainable expansion plan that kept our core values intact. I showed how our commitment to local partnerships actually increased guest loyalty and brand value. I prioritized investors who shared our values, rather than just those offering the most money.

For Regulators: I ensured full compliance with labor laws, safety regulations, and sustainability practices—not just to avoid fines, but to build a responsible business. We joined green tourism initiatives and voluntarily exceeded environmental regulations.

For Industry Leaders: I engaged in hospitality forums and leadership events, making Mirabelle known as a pioneer in experience-driven boutique hotels. We built partnerships with tourism boards, hospitality schools, and travel networks.

For Community Leaders: We hired locally and ensured fair wages. We participated in city events and local business programs. We supported cultural preservation efforts rather than imposing a generic, globalized hotel model.

The result? Mirabelle wasn't just a business—it became a respected institution.

Final Lesson: Align Expectations Without Compromising Vision

Understanding key decision-makers' expectations is about finding balance.

- *Investors want profit*—but businesses thrive when they also have purpose.
- *Regulators want compliance*—but businesses gain trust by exceeding expectations.
- *Industry leaders want innovation*—but success comes from staying true to your strengths.
- *Communities want respect*—but lasting success comes from shared prosperity.

At Mirabelle, we learned that aligning with decision-makers doesn't mean giving up your values—it means proving that your values are what make the business valuable. The best businesses don't just meet expectations; they set new standards.

Foresee Probable Future Expectations

At first, I believed running a hotel meant perfecting the present—delivering seamless check-ins, warm hospitality, and unforgettable stays. But as Mirabelle grew, I realized that hospitality wasn't just about meeting current expectations—it was about anticipating the future. Guests' needs evolved, industry trends shifted, and societal expectations kept changing. If I wanted Mirabelle to not just survive, but thrive, I had to stay ahead of the curve.

Identifying Emerging Trends

While thinking about emerging trends, I asked myself:

- What will guests expect a year from now?
- Five years?
- A decade?

To anticipate shifts, I:

Monitored Industry Reports—Followed hospitality trends through reports, conferences, and expert analyses.

Engaged with Guests—Conducted surveys and informal chats to understand their evolving needs.

Observed Competitors and Innovators—Learned from businesses setting new standards in guest experience.

One evening, while chatting with a frequent guest, she casually mentioned: "I love your hotel, but I wish check-in was faster. Sometimes, after a long flight, all I want is to go straight to my room." That was my lightbulb moment. Within six months, we introduced digital check-ins and keyless entry, ensuring guests could check in instantly via their phones.

The feedback was overwhelmingly positive, and soon, other hotels followed our lead.

Predicting Guest Needs Before They Voice Them

Rather than waiting for guests to request changes, I proactively designed solutions. For instance, I noticed an increasing demand for wellness experiences—people were seeking calm in their travels. Instead of waiting for feedback, we introduced mindfulness spaces in the hotel, organic dining options curated by local nutritionists, and personalized wellness programs, including yoga and meditation sessions. Guests loved it—it wasn't just a hotel stay anymore; it was a retreat for their mind and body.

Instead of guessing what guests might want in the future, we integrated AI-powered data analytics to track emerging trends: AI analyzes booking patterns to predict future demand., sentiment analysis scans social media reviews to detect changing preferences, and predictive pricing models adjust room rates dynamically.

By leveraging technology, we anticipated customer needs before they even voiced them.

Aligning with Societal and Environmental Changes

Future expectations weren't just about guest preferences—they were about broader social and environmental responsibilities.

Sustainability: Guests expected green initiatives, so we invested in:

- Solar energy and water-saving systems
- Zero-waste programs and plastic-free packaging
- Local, ethical sourcing for food and supplies

Labor Practices: Instead of waiting for laws to push us, we adopted:

- Fair employment policies and inclusive hiring
- Employee well-being and mental health programs

Accessibility: We ensured:

- All rooms, facilities, and technology were fully accessible

- Adaptive technology was integrated for guests with disabilities

By integrating these early, we weren't just compliant—we were leading the way.

Future-Proofing the Business Model

To ensure that Mirabelle remained relevant, I built adaptability into our business model:

Flexible Room Designs—Spaces that could be repurposed for different guest needs (business, leisure, wellness retreats).

Tech Integration—Investing in AI-powered guest experiences before they became industry standards.

Loyalty Beyond Discounts—Creating community-driven loyalty programs based on personalized experiences, not just pricing incentives.

One evening, I overheard a guest say: "This hotel knows just what I need, even before I do." That was when I knew Mirabelle wasn't just reacting to change—it was shaping the future of hospitality.

Final Lesson: Businesses That Predict the Future Create It

If you want to lead, you can't just meet today's expectations—you must anticipate tomorrow's. You can do this:

- Observe market leaders and industry disruptors.
- Monitor technology trends and regulatory changes.
- Listen to your customers—not just to what they say, but to what they will need.

The best businesses don't just react to change—they define it.

Ways to Understand Expectations of Interest Groups

When I first opened Mirabelle, I assumed that if I provided great service and comfortable rooms, success would follow naturally. But I quickly learned that running a hotel isn't about what I think is important—it's about what my guests, employees, partners, and the community expect.

People don't always tell you what they need. Sometimes, they don't even know how to put it into words. I had to find ways to listen beyond words—to truly understand what my interest groups expected, even before they voiced it.

Direct Engagement and Open Conversations

One evening, I sat across from a longtime guest, Mr. Omar, as he sipped his usual cup of mint tea in the lounge.

"How's your stay?" I asked.

"As good as always," he replied.

A safe answer. But I pushed further, "If you could change one thing about your experience here, what would it be?"

He hesitated, then shrugged. "I suppose I'd like a quieter space to unwind. The lounge is great, but sometimes, I just want a place with fewer distractions." That was something he had never mentioned before.

The next month, we created a private relaxation lounge—a tucked-away space with soft lighting, calming music, and cozy reading nooks. The first guest to use it? Mr. Omar.

"This is exactly what I needed. I just didn't know how to say it," he told me.

That conversation taught me a valuable lesson: people don't always directly state their expectations—but if you ask the right questions, you can uncover what truly matters.

Observing Behavior and Analyzing Data

Not all expectations are spoken out loud. Sometimes, you have to watch and listen differently. Instead of just reading guest reviews, I started observing guest behavior: Which services did they use most? What were they avoiding? What did their body language say about their experience?

I noticed that business travelers tended to leave early and skip breakfast. Instead of waiting for complaints, we introduced grab-and-go breakfast options. Within a month, guest satisfaction scores improved significantly.

For employees, I looked beyond surveys and noticed: Were people leaving their jobs too quickly? Were they engaging in team meetings or staying silent?

When I saw that our housekeeping team had the highest turnover, I didn't just increase salaries—I introduced flexible shifts and well-being programs. The result? Retention skyrocketed.

Data doesn't just confirm what you already know—it reveals things you might have overlooked.

Industry Benchmarking and Competitive Insights

I wasn't just learning from my own hotel—I was watching the best in the industry. I asked myself:

- What were leading hotels doing differently?
- What were customers raving about in competitor reviews?
- How could Mirabelle set a new standard?

When I saw that luxury hotels were investing in AI-powered concierge services, I didn't wait for it to become mainstream—I implemented an AI-driven guest assistant before my competitors.

When I noticed that eco-conscious travelers were favoring sustainable stays, I didn't just install energy-efficient lighting—we built a full-scale zero-waste program and partnered with local farmers for organic dining.

Learning from the best meant we were never playing catch-up—we were leading the way.

Leveraging Technology for Real-Time Insights

I realized that in today's world, technology could help us listen better, and we implemented:

Social Media Listening—Monitoring what guests were saying about us online, even if they didn't tag us.

AI-Powered Feedback Analysis—Analyzing reviews across platforms to identify common themes.

Real-Time Guest Surveys—Short, one-question check-ins instead of lengthy feedback forms.

One evening, our AI analysis flagged a small but consistent complaint—guests found our hallway lighting too dim at night. We adjusted the lighting, and within weeks, guests started commenting on how much safer and more comfortable the hotel felt.

The key takeaway? People will always tell you what they need—you just have to listen in the right ways.

Monitoring Competitors: A Hidden Interest Group

I used to think competitors had nothing to do with my business—but I quickly learned that their actions influence guest expectations too. If a competitor launched a new loyalty program, guests expected something similar from us. If a major hotel chain improved sustainability efforts, eco-conscious travelers would compare our commitment. If a competitor invested in smart-room technology, guests would assume we should have it too.

Instead of seeing competitors as a threat, I saw them as a source of intelligence. By anticipating their moves and staying ahead, Mirabelle remained a leader—not a follower.

Final Lesson: People's Needs Aren't Always Loud—But They're Always There

I used to believe that guests, employees, and partners would clearly communicate their expectations, but over time, I learned that people don't always say what they need—you have to listen between the lines. Behavior tells you just as much as words. Looking outside your business helps you stay ahead, and technology can help you understand expectations in real time.

Using a mix of direct conversations, behavioral analysis, industry insights, and technology-driven monitoring, I was able to anticipate expectations before they became demands. That's how Mirabelle didn't just meet expectations—it exceeded them.

Analyze the Overall Situation for Potential Risks

It was late at night, and I was sitting in my office at Mirabelle, flipping through our latest reports. Occupancy rates were high. Customer satisfaction was solid. Revenue was growing steadily. On the surface, everything seemed perfect. But I couldn't shake the feeling that something was missing. That evening, I had read an article about a well-known hotel chain that had suddenly lost half its bookings after a social media scandal. It wasn't the scandal itself that caught my attention—it was the speed at which everything fell apart. One mistake. One miscalculation. One overlooked risk, and suddenly, a thriving business can crumble.

That night, I asked myself: *What are the hidden risks in my business that I'm not seeing?*

Identifying Potential Risks Before They Become Problems

I started breaking down every part of my business, asking:

Guest Experience Risks: Were there service inconsistencies that could lead to bad reviews?

Operational Risks: What would happen if our supply chain was disrupted?

Financial Risks: Were we too dependent on a single revenue stream?

Regulatory Risks: Were we staying ahead of evolving laws and compliance requirements?

Reputational Risks: Could a misunderstanding or negative review spiral out of control?

Technology Risks: Were guest data and payment systems secure against cyber threats?

The deeper I looked, the more I realized how many hidden risks existed beneath the surface.

Learning from Experience: The Overbooking Crisis

One of my first big risk-related mistakes happened in our second year. We had just partnered with a major travel booking platform, and reservations shot up overnight. At first, it felt like a huge win. Until we realized… A technical glitch had overbooked our rooms during a major event weekend.

That night, I had to personally face angry guests who had arrived, only to find no available rooms. It was one of the worst nights of my career. But I learned from it. I introduced real-time inventory tracking to avoid system errors; I added an automatic buffer to prevent overbooking; and I trained my team on how to handle booking issues with empathy and solutions.

Since that day, we never had an overbooking crisis again. The lesson? Risks aren't just threats—they're lessons waiting to be learned.

Scenario Planning: Preparing for the Unexpected

After handling an overbooking crisis, I built a habit of "scenario planning"— preparing for possible risks before they happened.

What if we had a sudden revenue drop? We built a financial reserve and diversified income streams.

What if key suppliers failed to deliver? We developed backup partnerships to avoid disruptions.

What if there was a PR crisis? We created a crisis communication plan to respond quickly and professionally.

This kind of thinking changed the way I ran my business. Instead of just reacting to problems, I started anticipating and preventing them.

Using Data and Team Insights to Spot Weaknesses

To improve our ability to identify risks early, I introduced a few key things:

Guest Trend Analysis—Watching for small dips in guest satisfaction before they became big issues.

Employee Feedback Loops—Encouraging employees to report operational concerns before they escalated.

Competitor Monitoring—Learning from mistakes made by others in the industry.

I noticed that our sustainability efforts were falling behind compared to competitors. Travelers were becoming more eco-conscious, and some had started choosing other hotels because we weren't fully aligned with their values.

We responded before it became a problem, accelerating our sustainability initiatives by implementing zero-waste programs in guest services, energy-efficient rooms powered by renewable sources, and ethical sourcing for food and amenities.

Within months, we regained our competitive edge—before we had lost too many guests. The lesson? The best way to see risks coming is to listen—to customers, to employees, to the market.

The Risk Classification Framework

To stay organized, we introduced a Risk Matrix to classify risks based on impact and probability:

Risk Type	Impact	Probability	Action Plan
Supply chain disruption	High	Medium	Secure backup suppliers
PR crisis from negative reviews	Medium	High	Proactive reputation management
Employee retention issues	High	High	Improve workplace culture and benefits
Cybersecurity threat	High	Medium	Invest in stronger data protection

By classifying risks this way, we focused on the biggest threats first. Instead of reacting, we stayed ahead.

Managing Risky Expectations

Not every expectation from interest groups can—or should—be met. Some expectations are risky and need careful handling.

Success-related risks: A competitor expected us to lower prices aggressively—but doing so would hurt our profitability. Instead, we focused on added value rather than discounts.

Operational risks: Employees wanted full remote work, but certain roles required on-site presence. We implemented a hybrid model to balance flexibility with business needs.

Financial risks: Suppliers wanted extended payment terms, but we had to protect cash flow. We negotiated long-term agreements with structured payments.

Regulatory risks: Some groups expected faster product launches, but rushing would have compromised safety and compliance. We stuck to our high ethical standards.

The key? Communicating these decisions openly so that no group felt ignored or dismissed.

Final Lesson: Stay Ahead of Risks, Don't Just React

I used to think risk management was about fixing problems when they happened. But now I know: It's about seeing trouble before it arrives and being ready.

- If you don't look for risks, you won't see them coming.
- If you wait until a crisis happens, you're already too late.
- If you think you're safe, you're probably missing something.

Because in business, the biggest risk is thinking that nothing can go wrong.

At Mirabelle, we don't wait for problems to find us—we find them first and stop them in their tracks. That's how we ensure that success isn't just built—it's protected.

Resolve Serious Conflicts in the Overall Situation

It started with a simple disagreement—but it quickly grew into a major crisis. Our kitchen crew and suppliers were at odds over a sudden increase in food prices. Our longtime organic farm supplier raised their prices by 30% due to rising operational costs. My head chef, Luis, was furious.

"We can't afford this," he told me. "We'll either have to cut quality or raise menu prices—neither option is good for us."

But our supplier, Amara, was just as firm. "We're struggling too," she said. "If we lower our prices, we won't survive."

Suddenly, everyone was feeling the impact. The kitchen team was worried about job security, guests started noticing smaller portions as the chefs cut costs, and tension between the team and the supplier grew—each blaming the other.

It was escalating fast. If I didn't intervene, this could damage our reputation as a boutique hotel known for quality, our employees' morale and job stability, and a key business relationship we had built over years. Something had to be done—but how?

Finding Common Ground: Understanding the Root of the Conflict

At first, it looked like just a pricing issue. But when I stepped back and listened, I realized that the supplier wasn't being unfair—they were struggling to stay afloat. The kitchen team wasn't just upset about costs— they were afraid guests would leave if prices went up. The real issue wasn't money—it was trust.

So, instead of making a rushed decision, I took three steps: I sat down with Luis (the head chef) to understand his concerns. I met with Amara (the supplier) to see if we could find common ground. I reviewed our finances to see where we had flexibility.

That's when I saw the bigger picture—this wasn't about picking a side. It was about finding a win-win solution that respected both our employees and our suppliers.

Finding a Win-Win Solution

Instead of taking the easy way out—either cutting costs recklessly or raising prices—we found a middle ground:

Phased Price Adjustment—Instead of an immediate 30% price increase, we agreed to a 15% increase now and another 15% in six months. This gave both sides time to adjust.

Operational Efficiency—We optimized our kitchen processes to reduce food waste, which helped offset some of the increased costs.

Menu Redesign—Instead of raising prices across the board, we introduced seasonal dishes using cost-effective, high-quality ingredients—keeping guests happy without major price hikes.

Long-Term Supplier Commitment—We formalized a multi-year contract with Amara's farm, ensuring future stability for both parties.

The Outcome: A Conflict That Made Us Stronger

After a conflict that ended with a win-win situation:

The supplier stayed in business—securing our supply chain.

Our kitchen team felt heard—no unnecessary layoffs, no panic.

Guests didn't feel the impact—and even loved the new seasonal menu.

Mirabelle strengthened a key relationship—instead of losing it.

The lesson? Conflict doesn't have to mean losing something—it can be an opportunity to build something better.

Leadership Lessons in Conflict Resolution

From this experience, I learned some of the most valuable leadership lessons of my career:

Listen Before You React—Most conflicts aren't about what they seem. Take time to understand the real problem.

Create Solutions, Not Sides—Conflict resolution isn't about "winning" or "losing"—it's about finding balance.

Think Long-Term, Not Short-Term—Rushed decisions can damage relationships. A well-thought-out approach builds trust and stability.

Communicate Openly—Fear and frustration grow when people feel unheard. Clear, honest conversations reduce uncertainty.

Not All Expectations Can Be Met—But they can be managed. The goal isn't to please everyone, but to find the best possible balance.

Other Common Conflicts and How to Balance Them

The Mirabelle kitchen conflict wasn't the only kind of conflicting interest groups face. Here are some other real-world conflicts and ways to handle them:

Shareholders vs. Employees

Shareholders want higher financial returns.

Employees want fair wages and job security.

Balanced Approach: Invest in employee development to boost productivity, which benefits both employees and investors.

Customers vs. Suppliers

Customers want lower prices and higher quality.

Suppliers want fair compensation for their goods.

Balanced Approach: Support suppliers in cost-reducing innovations without compromising product quality.

Investors vs. Society

Investors prioritize short-term profits.

Society expects ethical, sustainable business practices.

Balanced Approach: Show investors that sustainability efforts create long-term competitive advantages and brand trust.

The key? Every conflict can be turned into an opportunity—if handled with a plan, empathy, and transparency.

Final Lesson: Conflicts Can Strengthen a Business—If Handled Correctly

When I first faced this conflict, I felt stuck—like I had to choose sides. But in the end, I realized that great businesses aren't built by avoiding conflict—they are built by managing it wisely.

We didn't lose a supplier—we deepened a partnership. We didn't upset guests—we created a better dining experience. We didn't panic—we adapted, innovated, and came out stronger.

Conflict isn't a sign of failure—it's a chance to build something even better.

Don't Miss Last-minute Changes of Expectations

The reservation looked normal at first. VIP guest, three-night stay, premium suite. Nothing unusual. But an hour before check-in, my phone buzzed with an urgent message from the front desk. "Maya, the VIP guest just called. He's requesting a fully plant-based, locally sourced menu for his entire stay. He assumed we already had this option."

I blinked at the message. Assumed? Our kitchen offered vegetarian and vegan dishes, but a fully customized, locally sourced vegan menu—on such short notice? That was a different challenge. And this wasn't just any guest. He was a well-known travel influencer with hundreds of thousands of followers.

If we got this wrong, it wouldn't just be one unhappy guest—it could be a PR nightmare. I took a deep breath. We needed a plan. Fast.

The Fast-Paced Solution: Turning a Crisis into an Opportunity

Step 1: Rallying the Team

I called an emergency meeting with the kitchen crew and restaurant manager.

"We don't have time to panic," I said. "We have time to prepare. What can we do with what we already have?"

Luis, our chef, rubbed his chin. "We can adjust some dishes, but if we want it to feel special, we need better ingredients."

"Then let's get them," I said. "We have two hours."

Step 2: Finding a Creative Solution

Fast Local Sourcing—We partnered with a nearby organic grocer who could deliver fresh ingredients within an hour.

Smart Menu Tweaks—Instead of creating a whole new menu from scratch, we modified our best dishes, ensuring that they remained local, fresh, and plant-based.

Elevated Presentation—We trained the waiters quickly to explain the ingredients and origins of each dish, turning it into a unique guest experience rather than a last-minute scramble.

Step 3: Delivering an Unforgettable Experience

By the time our VIP guest arrived, his custom menu was ready—down to the locally sourced herbal tea selection.

We didn't just meet his expectations, we exceeded them. Later that evening, he posted a raving review on social media:

"The best plant-based dining experience I've ever had at a boutique hotel."

The post went viral.

Within a week, we received 30+ new reservations from guests requesting our plant-based dining experience. What started as a last-minute challenge became one of Mirabelle's signature offerings.

The Business Truth: Expectations Can Change Instantly

If there's one thing I've learned in the hospitality business, it's this: People's needs change fast.

A guest who was excited yesterday might have an entirely different need today.

An employee who seemed content last month might be considering leaving today.

A business partnership that felt secure might suddenly be on shaky ground.

The real challenge isn't just meeting expectations—it's keeping up when they shift unexpectedly.

How to Catch Last-Minute Expectation Changes

That experience changed the way I approached last-minute shifts in expectations. Now, I have a system in place to anticipate and respond quickly.

1. Monitor Guest and Interest Group Behavior in Real Time: Track guest social media posts, special requests, and past preferences to detect changes in their needs.

Example: If a returning guest suddenly prefers non-alcoholic drinks, we adjust the minibar before they arrive.

2. Maintain a Flexible Team Mindset: Hold regular "expectation check-ins" with employees, suppliers, and partners.

Example: If a corporate group decides last minute to hold an impromptu networking event, we ensure that the lounge is set up within the hour.

3. Have Contingency Plans: Prepare pre-planned responses for common last-minute changes.

Example: If a VIP requests a private car service last-minute, we have priority partnerships with a local provider for instant availability.

4. Use AI and Technology for Real-Time Early Warnings: Social Media Listening—We monitor what guests are saying online, even if they don't tag us.

AI-Powered Feedback Analysis—We analyze reviews across platforms to identify common trends before they escalate.

Predictive Analytics—AI tracks booking patterns and guest behaviors to predict potential expectation shifts.

The Early Warning System: Staying Ahead of Expectation Changes

Beyond customers, last-minute expectation changes happen across all interest groups:

Employees—Workplace culture and job expectations shift. Regular check-ins prevent talent loss.

Partners and Suppliers—Market disruptions can change delivery timelines. Real-time tracking prevents supply chain failures.

Society—Social and environmental expectations evolve. Monitoring public sentiment protects reputation.

Key Decision-Makers—New regulations and policies can appear overnight. Early intelligence ensures compliance.

Competitors—Their strategies influence market trends. Smart tracking keeps us ahead.

The best early warning systems detect real-time change signals using a combination of human insight and AI-powered analytics. The faster we adapt, the bigger our competitive advantage.

Final Lesson: Success Is in the Details—Especially the Last-Minute Ones

I used to think success came from long-term planning. Now I know success comes from long-term planning AND last-minute agility. People's expectations aren't fixed. They shift with trends, they evolve with experiences, and they change overnight. If you're not paying attention, you'll get left behind.

At Mirabelle, we don't just react—we anticipate. We don't see last-minute changes as inconveniences—we see them as opportunities to impress. Because, at the end of the day, the guests who say "This hotel just gets me" aren't just satisfied—they become loyal for life.

Chapter Three

Embrace Balanced Planning (STEP 3)

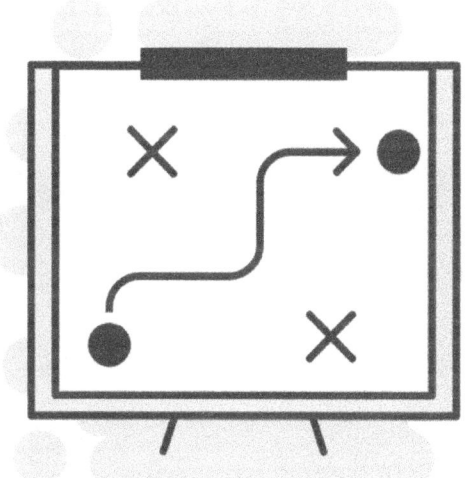

With the KAIZUNO method, a well-thought-out plan helps you achieve your goals and meet all relevant expectations of your interest groups in a balanced way. A good plan creates benefits for all and avoids unnecessary effort—because no one wants to waste time or resources toward success.

A realistic plan that fits smoothly into your daily routines provides clarity and security, and can be easily communicated and implemented. If things don't go as expected, you can adjust your course flexibly and still stay on track to achieve your success goals.

Have Good Answers to the Expectations of Your Interest Groups

When planning, you decide which expectations you want to fulfill and which not. Your target picture will help you with this decision. The simplest recipe for a good plan that leads to success is to find good answers to the expectations you want to fulfill. The consolidated portfolio of interest group expectations is a strong, solid, and robust fundament for your success planning. A good plan should be attractive, balanced, and free of contradictions.

Your leadership challenge is to define a well-balanced plan that provides good answers to all your interest groups. This increases the probability of you satisfying all your interest groups at the same time. That is at least the vision.

Know How to Satisfy Your Customers

Your plan to satisfy your customers could include high-level statements related to ways how you:

- Further improve the collaboration with them.
- Work with them at an even higher trust level.
- Provide more sustainable value to them.
- Offer a larger variety of products and services.
- Provide more competitive pricing for selected products and services.
- Increase their overall experience with your products and services.

Know How to Satisfy Your Employees

Your plan to satisfy your employees could include high-level statements related to ways how you:

- Further improve their working environment.
- Support team work more actively.
- Offer more career opportunities.
- Offer more opportunities to share experience and learning.
- Introduce a larger variety of recognition of outstanding performance.
- Provide more options to increase work-life balance.

Know How to Satisfy Your Partners and Suppliers

Your plan to satisfy your partners and suppliers could include high-level statements related to ways how you:

- Enable better collaboration on the design of products and services.
- Involve them deeper in your high-level decisions.
- Increase purchasing volumes due to more customer business.
- Increase your support regarding the decarbonization of the whole supply chain.
- Offer to tap more on their expertise to increase customer experience with their contribution.

Know How to Satisfy Society

Your plan to satisfy society could include high-level statements related to ways how you:

- Speed up the implementation of sustainable energy supplies.
- Further improve the levels of recycling and reuse at production.

- Reduce the overall environmental footprint of your operations through cleaner technologies and smarter resource use.
- Encourage diversity, equity, and inclusion policies even more.
- Support community projects more actively.

Know How to Satisfy Key Decision-Makers

Your plan to satisfy key decision-makers could include high-level statements related to ways how you:

- Further improve trust by enhancing transparency and accountability.
- Provide online access to real-time dashboards of key information.
- Proactively implement new regulations on sustainability.
- Further improve relationships with your governance.
- Use better digital ways of communication.

Know How to Achieve Success with a Good Plan

To get closer to your target picture, you need a well-balanced, consistent, convincing, overarching plan. A high-level plan (imagine an airplane at 30,000 feet) helps you see the essential elements you should fulfill for success, without being distracted by too many details. A good plan provides clarity, connects success goals with the expectations of key interest groups, and ensures that resources are used in a targeted manner. If your plan is perceived as attractive and promising, support and motivation for implementation by your interest groups increase.

Note: Your plan toward the target picture can also be called the "Strategy". We decided to stay with the term "Plan" in this book since it is easier to understand. After all, we use plans in our private lives all the time, but we rarely talk about strategies in our family.

Why Success Requires Good Planning

If you want to achieve any goal successfully, it is much easier to get there with a good plan. Humans are constantly planning everything, even unconsciously. How you want to organize your day, how you want to deal with your fellow human beings, how you want to organize the dog when you are away, where and how you want to spend your vacations, and what you want to take on vacation for what purposes and for what weather.

For your private planning, it is fine to sit down at the kitchen table for a short time and discuss things with the family, just with a piece of paper and a pen. Planning is natural and does not necessarily require a great deal of effort. Only for larger, important and long-term projects, like building a house, you plan in a more systematic way.

The same principles apply to planning in your organizational context. Even small organizations discuss numerous plans at the same time. If these plans are not consolidated into an overarching plan, this can lead to conflicts of interest between the individual plans, e.g., regarding resources.

Successful organizations have individual plans for all their interest groups, and an overarching plan that ensures that all individual plans are well-related, consolidated, and interconnected. This ensures that the available resources are used efficiently and that success is achieved in a balanced way across all plans. This also guarantees that the overall plan can be effectively implemented in a coordinated way, in order to achieve consistent success.

Critical Success Factors

When organizations define their success goals and related plans based on harmonized interest group expectations, some add an intermediate step: they define critical success factors before they define goals. This step can be beneficial, as these critical success factors can help define success goals more precisely.

For example, if customers want faster service, this expectation could be swiftly translated into the success goal: "Reduce service time by 30%

in 4 months". Alternatively, a related critical success factor—"improve operational efficiency"—could be defined first. This could lead to a more precise success goal: "Reduce response time by 30% by improving logistics and automation within 4 months".

Critical success factors can help filter expectations of interest groups and make it easier for organizations to focus on what truly drives success. This can prevent getting lost in too many unspecific goals, while ensuring clarity and direction toward success.

Define Suitable Success Goals

Success goals provide orientation and show what matters. Without goals, it remains unclear what you want to achieve and how you progress toward success. Success goals help leaders to make the right decisions.

Good success goals are specific, measurable, achievable, relevant and time-bound (SMART). Here are some examples.

For customers: Expand the product assortment on our online sales platform by introducing 50 new consumer product stock keeping units within 6 months, and increase variety by 20% to meet customer demand for more choices.

For employees: Implement 5 new part-time shift schedules in the production department within 2 months, ensuring all employees can choose from at least 8 shift options to improve flexibility and work-life balance.

For partners and suppliers: Increase the purchasing volume of raw materials and pre-production components from our top 3 suppliers by 15% within 6 months to enhance supply chain stability and meet growing production demands.

For society: Increase the proportion of renewable energy sources used in production from 27% to 35% within 4 months by integrating solar and wind energy contracts, reducing the company's carbon footprint.

For key decision-makers: Deploy a fully functional, cloud-based digital dashboard within 7 months and granting **real-time access** to key decision-makers across all departments for improved data-driven decision-making.

While it makes sense to structure your success goals according to your interest groups (who shared their expectations before in the same structure), it is important that your leaders review all success goals before they finalize them, to ensure that they create an overall harmonious picture.

Individual success goals should always support and never contradict each other. Only if this principle is fulfilled will the following implementation work smoothly.

Note: We use "success goals" here instead of "strategic goals" to emphasize the important correlation between these goals and success, which is created through implementation of goals through processes. But this is just terminology. Please keep using the term strategic goals if you wish.

Note: Some organizations define "strategic initiatives" as high-level projects. There is a lot of confusion about this practice, even in world-renowned international organizations. In particular, strategic projects are often confused with processes. How can strategic initiatives/projects support your journey toward success?

Basically, projects can be defined on a low (operational or process) or high (planning or strategic) level.

You will implement your success plan in STEP 4 with processes. If any of these processes have to be improved due to performance problems, a process improvement project is started. This low-level, operational project is terminated as soon as the improvement goal for the related process has been achieved.

Strategic initiatives are high-level projects, defined to improve an overarching aspect that has critical influence on the success of the organization. As soon as project-related success goals have been achieved, the strategic initiative is terminated. Examples of strategic initiatives/projects could be:

- Leveraging big data and AI to analyze customer preferences and behavior for hyper-personalized marketing.

- Applying lean principles and robotic process automation to improve production efficiency and reduce waste.

- Strengthening cybersecurity infrastructure to protect customer and business data.

- Implementing sustainable business practices to meet ESG (environmental, social and governance) sustainability goals.

- Strengthening diversity, equity and inclusion policies and implement them in hiring and leadership training.

Focus on Success, Then on Performance

Every organization wants to be successful. Therefore, they define success goals and try hard to achieve them. Success is the most important goal for organizations, because only sustainable success secures the future. However, organizations who achieve similar success with less effort have a competitive advantage on the market. Less effort, costs and resources mean higher performance (or efficiency).

What is more important? Certainly success. Without success, performance does not really matter. Focus on success first, then on performance. The best organizations manage to optimize both success and performance, and achieve the best possible balance between the two factors.

While we keep focusing on success in this STEP, we will explain performance in STEP 4.

Ensure the Feasibility of Your Plan

A good plan must be feasible and realistic. Only then does it fulfill the basic requirements for implementation. To create a feasible plan takes time and resources. Depending on the ambitions of your plan, the requirements may be higher or lower.

To achieve your success goals, you need an overarching master plan that includes all the necessary individual plans, e.g., for each of the relevant interest groups. The common basis for all these plans are the expectations of interest groups, which were collected, consolidated, and harmonized in STEP 2.

To implement these plans, you need an implementation plan that defines how, when and by what means your plans are to be implemented to achieve success.

Here are key criteria that ensure that plans can be successfully implemented in practice:

1. Alignment with Organizational Capabilities

- Implementation must match the available employees, talents, and resources.
- Implementation must take into account existing processes and infrastructure.
- Complexity and overall cost should not grow through implementation.

Example: A manufacturing firm planning to implement AI-driven automation must ensure that existing production lines are compatible with the new technology and operators have required skills and competencies.

2. Operational Feasibility

- Implementation must translate into actionable steps.
- Implementation plans need ownership and each implementation step needs clear accountability.
- Implementation should fit within existing processes, or enhance them.

Example: If your plan involves expanding to new international markets, there should be clear steps for supply chain adjustments, compliance with new local regulations, marketing localization and hiring regional sales teams.

3. Financial Feasibility

- The organization must have the financial capacity to support the implementation.
- Implementation plans should balance cost vs. benefit and have a positive financial impact after implementation (return on investment or ROI).
- Financial planning should account for potential financial risks, e.g., unexpected costs.

Example: If a company wants to increase sustainability by switching to renewable energy, they must assess upfront costs of installation, possible resistance from local communities, and also long-term cost savings.

4. Interest Groups Buy-In and Engagement

- Implementation plans should incorporate input from all relevant interest groups before execution.
- Implementation plans must be openly communicated with all relevant interest groups to ensure understanding, engagement and support.
- To improve the probability of success, implementation plans should be supported by change management initiatives.

Example: A company implementing a digital transformation plan should ensure that IT, operations, people, and talent management are aligned, and all affected interest groups understand the benefits of that transformation.

5. Risk Management and Agility

- Implementation plans must be subject to comprehensive risk management, including risk analysis and assessment, countermeasures, emergency, crisis and continuity management.

- Implementation plans need to be flexible and agile to be adapted quickly to changes that may arise as a surprise during implementation.

- Alternative implementation plans should be available in case the original plan faces obstacles or disruptions.

Example: If a company plans to launch a new product line, it should account for supply chain risks, customer adoption challenges, regulatory hurdles, or competitive responses.

6. Implementation Timeline and Progress Tracking

- Implementation plans need milestones, responsibilities and deliverables.

- Progress tracking should ensure that implementation deliverables are achieved on time and in budget.

- Clear termination criteria should be defined if achievement of expected success turns out to be impossible, to avoid waste of time, people and resources.

Example: During the implementation of a digital transformation plan, it becomes clear that key customers do not accept the digital solution. In this case, the implementation must be canceled immediately. A new plan must take better account of customer expectations.

"Everything conceived must one day pass through reality."

—Albert Einstein

Ensure Your Plan Is Risk-tested

Most organizations limit risk management to operational risks or obvious external risks such as:

- Market volatility: rapid changes in markets with critical impact on customer demand.

- Natural disasters: events such as floods, fires or earthquakes.

- Political or social instability: Events like strikes, protests or policy changes affecting supply chains or operations.

- Financial risks: Insolvency of key customers, suppliers or partners, or tax related risks.

Only few consider other substantial risks related to *internal disruptions* such as:

- Loss of key decision-makers or key talents

- Massive quality incidents or accidents

- Loss of critical knowledge through acts of theft by internal people, employees with critical knowledge leaving or significant turnover

- Gross communication or marketing mistakes, e.g., following incidents or accidents

- Bad merger or acquisition decisions *(the failure rate of M&A projects ranges from 50% to 70%, depending on the specific metrics used to define failure)*

External disruptions such as:

- Massive cybersecurity breaches, e.g., by unauthorized access to sensitive data, causing loss of critical data and disrupting business continuity
- Large supply chain disruptions, causing shortage of key supply
- Significant changes in politics, legislation or regulations (e.g., USA in 2025)
- Unexpected disruptions in general health (e.g., COVID-19 in 2020) or technology (e.g., DeepSeek in 2025)
- Unexpected hostile competitor actions

The impact of those risk events on organizations can easily have serious financial implications and disrupt business continuity, but it can also jeopardize the organizations' carefully crafted image and reputation. This is why it is absolutely mandatory to ensure that your plan is risk-tested. Before we show you how you can do that, we explain the basics of risk management.

Risk Management Basics

Professional risk management allows you to:

1. Identify, assess, and classify potential risks
2. Define effective measures to prevent risks
3. Reduce probability and impact of residual risks to an acceptable level
4. Proactively define emergency and crisis management
5. Ensure business continuity management.

To understand the importance of professional risk management for any responsible organization, just consider this little case study.

An international producer of baby food changes the supplier for their glass containers as part of a cost-savings plan that was proposed by a consultant. That change of supply causes a fault in production, which contaminates a large batch of containers with little, sharp glass splinters. Until the mistake gets discovered, tens of thousands of baby food containers are on the way to end-consumers.

Here is how professional risk management works in this case. There are 5 fundamental principles:

1. You can only avoid risk events if you foresee that might happen. A comprehensive risk register includes all potential risks that could probably happen to your organization, even very unlikely ones. There is lots of good practice information on risk registers publicly available that can serve as a benchmark.

   The organization's risk management team classifies—aided by AI-supported risk management software—all those potential risks according to a) their probability of occurrence and b) the impact they would cause. Consider that there are potential risks that may happen only very rarely, but cause immense impact, and vice versa, so these two dimensions are completely independent of each other. You may start with the most dangerous risk events (high probability and high impact) to implement principle #2.

2. Consider any proactive measures you have already in place to prevent those risks, or mitigate their damage. Fire extinguishers can reduce the damage caused by fires, but not their probability of occurrence. Classify these proactive measures according to their effectiveness. How much do these preventive measures reduce probability or impact? Since you will probably always detect residual risks, i.e., risks that are low but still exist despite preventive measures, move on to principle #3.

3. Consider how you can further reduce the probability and/or impact of those residual risks. Fire awareness and prevention education can reduce the probability of fires, while evacuation drills and exercises on how to operate fire extinguishers can reduce the impact of a potential fire. Implement those additional preventive measures and calculate the risk of fire again. Is there still a residual risk? Then think of further preventive measures.

Since it is almost impossible to reduce any risk probability and impact to zero, move on to principle #4.

4. Proactively define emergency and crisis management, just in case risks might happen, despite all prevention and precaution. While emergency management focuses on immediate, life-threatening situations, crisis management minimizes long-term damage to the organization's reputation, stability and future operations.

   Emergency and crisis management include organizational measures (e.g., defining a small but competent team of emergency and crisis officers who can act 24/7 if needed) and the definition and documentation of instructions for appropriate action in emergency and crisis situations. Eventually, the crisis will be over, but your organization is still in an exceptional state. This is why you need to prepare principle #5.

5. Business continuity management focuses on ensuring that an organization can maintain critical operations and quickly recovers from disruptions, thereby minimizing financial, operational and reputational damage. The goal is to bring operation back into a "normal" situation.

Now, let's apply these 5 risk management principles to our case study, the producer of baby food:

1. During a comprehensive risk analysis exercise, leaders discover the (very unlikely) risk event that due to a mistake in production, glass splinters or other foreign material could contaminate their baby food. They quickly agree that this event could be disastrous for the reputation of their organization and could even be an existential threat.

2. They review quality management and quality control of their production, and interfaces to their supply chain for glass containers. During that diligent analysis, they detect an issue at the interface between production and supply, and fix it.

3. The result of the latest analysis confirms that now all related processes are so safe and robust that the probability of such a risk event is very low. But since the impact of this event—should it happen against all odds—could be substantial, they plan principles #4 and #5 proactively.

4. They set up detailed emergency and crisis management that includes a diligently planned communication campaign; in case baby food is contaminated, every minute counts to warn distributors, shops, and end-users. This campaign includes all relevant communication channels and social media, and is "ready to be started" within 15 minutes by the emergency and crisis management team.

5. As a last risk management activity, business continuity management is planned, to bring production, sales, distribution and all other activities back to "normal" within a short time.

Needless to add, any risk register (the portfolio of potential risk events) needs to be constantly updated. This is why professional risk management systems include automatic scans of worldwide news for new incidents and accidents in real time, and some can do this sector specific. On that basis of past events, embedded AI can predict further potential events and simulate their potential impact. Subsequently, risk registers will be automatically updated and the risk management team will get an alert, so they can review and update existing risk calculations aided by risk management software.

This is how organizations ensure maximum protection. Unfortunately, even the most sophisticated AI-supported technology cannot predict and avoid all risks; there will always be residual risks to consider. The global COVID-19 pandemic may act as a permanent reminder.

Select the Best Risk Scenario for Your Plans

You can now apply the risk management philosophy to check the risks of your plans by asking:

1. What are potential risks for your organization or your interest groups if you implement your plans?

2. How can you prevent or reduce those risks by adjusting your plans?

3. How can you reduce probability and/or impact of residual risks of your plans to an acceptable level?

Since there might be more than one solution, this risk check will lead you to a few options or "scenarios" of your plans. Selecting the best possible scenario for your plans is a very challenging leadership task, since with your final plan you define nothing less than the future of your organization!

The result of this risk check should be the most riskless, robust, resilient, and sustainable version of your plans.

Be Flexible and Agile in Your Planning

Unfortunately, reality rarely adheres to a fixed plan. Unexpected developments can bring new opportunities or risks that you must respond to. A good plan considers various scenarios and allows for adjustments without losing sight of the success goal. It is particularly important to assess potential risks early and make provisions for unforeseen events. Different levels of flexibility are required, depending on the time horizon. While long-term plans provide orientation and stability, short-term plans must remain agile and be quick and easy to change.

Now, imagine you have defined your success plan on the basis of expectations and making it perfect and low-risk took a while. You have just decided for the best possible plan option (scenario) and you are ready for release, communication and implementation ... but suddenly your early warning system sends a red alert: one key expectation of a very important interest group just changed.

Example: As a car producer, you are dependent on emission regulations and limits. In a surprise move, the governmental regulator has just announced that he will reduce one of those limits much earlier than expected, due to a political change. This reduces the time to market with new engines dramatically. Your current plan for engine development and production has to be adjusted substantially. To keep your competitive position in the market, you need to be compliant with the new regulation faster than your competitor.

If your planning approach is tedious and complex, and if your plans have no built-in flexibility and agility, you have no chance to change it fast enough. This is why you need to create flexible, agile plans that can be easily and quickly adjusted.

This ability is a key competitive advantage that is often underestimated or even ignored by organizations.

"A dream without a plan is just a wish."

—Antoine de Saint-Exupéry

KAIZUNO teaches that true success requires structured yet flexible planning—where every decision is backed by feasibility, risk assessment, and strategic foresight.

Maya Dani had the vision, but did she have a plan? Without a solid plan, even the best ideas can crumble. Let's return to Maya's story.

Embrace Balanced Planning (STEP 3) - Application

Have good answers to the expectations of your interest groups

As Mirabelle grew, I realized that understanding expectations wasn't enough—I had to know how to respond to them effectively. Each interest group—customers, employees, partners and suppliers, society, and key decision-makers—had different priorities.

If I didn't have clear, confident answers to their concerns, I risked losing trust, damaging business relationships, and compromising long-term sustainability.

The Moment I Knew I Needed Better Answers

One morning, I sat down with a potential investor who was interested in funding our expansion. He leaned forward and asked, "How will Mirabelle stay competitive as bigger hotel brands expand in the city?"

I had a great vision, but in that moment, I realized that a vision wasn't enough. I needed specific, well-thought-out answers that demonstrated how we would differentiate ourselves, how we would stay profitable and sustainable, and how we would balance growth with our values.

That meeting changed my approach. From that day forward, I committed to always having good answers for every key interest group.

How I Built Clear, Strong Responses for Each Interest Group

Customers: "Why should I choose Mirabelle over other hotels?"

Answer: "We offer more than just a stay—we offer an experience. From curated city guides to personalized welcome notes, every guest feels at home."

Employees: "What career growth opportunities do I have here?"

Answer: "We believe in developing talent from within. We offer training programs, leadership mentoring, and promotion opportunities. Every employee is encouraged to grow with us."

Partners and Suppliers: "Why should we prioritize working with Mirabelle?"

Answer: "Because we believe in long-term partnerships, fair pricing, and mutual growth. We commit to supporting local suppliers, and our success means shared success."

Society: "How does Mirabelle contribute to the community and environment?"

Answer: "We invest in sustainability, source locally, and support social initiatives. Our zero-waste program and community projects ensure Mirabelle leaves a positive impact."

Key Decision-Makers: "How is Mirabelle ensuring compliance and responsible business practices?"

Answer: "We exceed regulatory standards in labor, environmental policies, and ethical sourcing. We proactively collaborate with authorities to lead industry best practices."

The Power of Having Good Answers

Once I started answering interest groups with clarity and confidence, three things happened:

Trust Increased: Employees, customers, partners and suppliers felt more secure in our vision.

Stronger Partnerships Formed: Investors, suppliers, and regulators saw us as a responsible business worth supporting.

Fewer Misunderstandings: Proactive communication reduced conflicts and confusion.

One day, an investor told me: "I've met many business owners with great ideas. But you? You have a plan. That's why I'm investing." That's when I knew—good answers don't just satisfy expectations; they build credibility and long-term success.

How a Balanced Plan Ensures Success for All Interest Groups

Customers—A strong plan improves collaboration, trust, and customer experience, leading to long-term loyalty.

Employees—A well-structured plan ensures career development, work-life balance, and a great work environment.

Partners and Suppliers—An effective plan creates better collaboration, innovation, and mutual growth.

Society—A sustainable plan contributes to environmental goals, community projects, and social equity.

Key Decision-Makers—A transparent plan enhances trust, compliance, and digital efficiency.

Final Lesson: Always Be Prepared to Answer "Why?"

Every business faces questions:

- Why should customers trust you?
- Why should employees stay loyal?
- Why should partners and suppliers collaborate with you?
- Why should society like your business?
- Why should key decision-makers support you?

The businesses that thrive are the ones that have strong, honest, and convincing answers. At Mirabelle, we don't just react to expectations—we prepare for them. Success isn't about knowing what interest groups expect—it's about being ready with the right response.

Know How to Achieve Success with a Good Plan

At first, I believed that passion and hard work were the keys to Mirabelle's success. I thought if I poured my heart into the hotel, everything would naturally fall into place. But I quickly learned that passion without a plan is wishful thinking. Running a successful business wasn't just about effort—it was about having a structured plan that connects vision, goals, and execution.

The Reality Check: Why Passion Alone Wasn't Enough

In my first year at Mirabelle, I worked harder than I ever had before: I greeted every guest personally. I monitored every review. I made sure every detail was perfect, but despite my effort, we faced cash flow problems—we were making money, but not managing it wisely; inconsistent bookings—some months were full, others were empty; operational inefficiencies—too much time was spent fixing problems instead of preventing them.

It wasn't that I wasn't working hard enough; I wasn't working *smart* enough. That's when I realized: Success isn't about doing more, it's about doing the right things in the right way.

I needed a clear, structured plan to ensure Mirabelle could thrive, not just survive.

The Key Elements of a Good Plan

I sat down and mapped out what a strong plan should include:

- *A Clear Vision and Goals*: What does success look like in 1 year? 5 years? 10 years?
- *Financial Stability*: How do we ensure profitability, manage costs, and maintain a steady cash flow?
- *Operational Efficiency*: How do we streamline processes to improve guest experience and minimize waste?
- *Customer and Market Strategy*: How do we attract and retain the right guests?
- *Risk Management*: How do we prepare for unexpected challenges?

Having a structured plan didn't mean things would always go as expected. But it meant that when challenges came, I had a roadmap to navigate them.

How I Built a Plan That Worked

Once I understood the importance of structured planning, I implemented key changes:

1. Creating Financial Stability:

- Built a budget that accounted for seasonal revenue fluctuations
- Negotiated better deals with partners and suppliers to improve profit margins
- Diversified income streams by offering event hosting, curated city tours, and long-term stays

2. Streamlining Operations:

- Created clear Standard Operating Procedures (SOPs) for consistent service quality
- Implemented training programs to empower employees and minimize inefficiencies
- Optimized housekeeping and front desk workflows to improve speed and guest experience

3. Building a Strong Customer and Market Plan:

- Focused on word-of-mouth marketing, encouraging guests to share their experiences
- Partnered with travel influencers to showcase Mirabelle as a unique destination
- Built a loyalty program to increase repeat bookings and guest retention

4. Preparing for Risks:

- Developed a crisis management plan for unexpected challenges (economic downturns, PR issues, operational disruptions)
- Created a financial reserve to handle emergencies

- Established backup partnerships with alternative suppliers to avoid service disruptions

The Impact: Why Planning Changed Everything

Once I had a structured plan in place, everything started to shift:

Profitability improved—we made smarter financial decisions.

Employee morale increased—a clear structure made work smoother.

Guest satisfaction grew—the experience felt effortless and well-managed.

I felt more in control—instead of reacting to problems, I was anticipating them.

One evening, a business consultant staying at Mirabelle told me: "Your hotel doesn't just feel welcoming—it feels like it runs with purpose. You can tell there's a solid plan behind everything."

That's when I knew—a good plan doesn't just create success; it makes success sustainable.

Final Lesson: Success is Built on Structure, Not Just Effort

I used to believe that success was about working harder—but now I know it's about working smarter.

- A vision without a plan is just a dream.
- A business without a plan is just gambling.
- Sustainable success comes from having a roadmap and executing it well.

At Mirabelle, we don't leave things to chance. We plan for success—and then we make it happen.

Define Suitable Success Goals

When I first opened Mirabelle, I had just one goal: survival, but as the hotel grew, I realized that survival wasn't enough. I needed to think beyond today—to define what success meant and plan how to achieve it. Success isn't about vague ambitions. It's about setting the right goals and knowing how to reach them.

The Mistake of Undefined Goals

At first, my goals were too broad:

I want Mirabelle to be successful.

I want more guests.

I want to expand someday.

These statements sounded great, but they lacked clarity.

How would I know if I was succeeding?

What did "more guests" really mean?

What kind of expansion was I aiming for?

Without specific goals, I was just hoping for success instead of planning for it.

Setting SMART Success Goals: A Game-Changer

I realized I needed to define success in a way that was actionable and measurable. That's when I started using the SMART goal framework:

Specific: Clearly define what I want to achieve.

Measurable: Set criteria for tracking progress.

Achievable: Ensure the goal is realistic.

Relevant: Align the goal with my overall business vision.

Time-bound: Set a deadline for achieving it.

For example:

I want more guests.

Increase occupancy from 75% to 90% over the next 12 months.

I want to expand someday.

Open a second Mirabelle location within 3 years, maintaining the same guest experience standards.

I want to improve customer satisfaction.

Increase guest ratings from 4.3 to 4.7 stars on major booking platforms by implementing personalized experiences and employee training within 9 months.

Defining Success Goals for Different Interest Groups

To create balanced success, I structured my goals based on the five key interest groups:

Customers: Ensuring Exceptional Experiences

- Increase repeat guest bookings by 25% in one year by launching a loyalty program.
- Reduce guest complaints by 30% in six months by refining service training and implementing real-time feedback loops.

Employees: Building a Strong Team

- Maintain an employee satisfaction rate of 85% through career development programs.

- Reduce employee turnover by 15% by implementing work-life balance initiatives and increasing internal promotion opportunities.

Partners and Suppliers: Strengthening Business Relationships

- Increase purchasing volume from top 3 suppliers by 15% within 6 months to enhance supply chain stability and meet growing demand.
- Reduce supplier delivery inconsistencies by 20% through structured quarterly reviews and performance incentives.

Society: Making a Positive Impact

- Increase the proportion of renewable energy used at Mirabelle from 40% to 60% in the next 18 months by integrating solar energy contracts.
- Host monthly community events to strengthen relationships with local businesses and cultural organizations.

Key Decision-Makers: Ensuring Sustainable Growth

- Deploy a cloud-based performance dashboard within 7 months to provide real-time operational insights to investors and decision-makers.
- Achieve a profit margin of 20% by the end of year three through cost optimization and revenue diversification.

The Impact: Why the Right Goals Changed Everything

Once I started setting well-defined success goals, I saw an immediate shift:

Clearer focus: Every decision aligned with measurable outcomes.

Stronger motivation: Employees had specific milestones to work toward.

Better financial planning: We knew exactly what revenue targets we needed to hit.

Faster growth: Instead of waiting for success, we created it.

One day, a guest asked me: "Maya, what's next for Mirabelle?"

And for the first time, I didn't have a vague answer—I had a clear plan.

Final Lesson: Define Your Destination Before You Start the Journey

If you don't define success, you'll never know when you've achieved it. Clear goals give your interest groups direction, motivation, and purpose. The right goals turn a dream into a plan—and a plan into reality and success.

At Mirabelle, we don't just aim for success. We define it, measure it, and achieve it—one goal at a time.

Focus on Success, Then on Performance

In the early days of Mirabelle, I was obsessed with daily performance metrics—occupancy rates, guest check-in times, and revenue per room. I believed that if we performed well every day, we would automatically become successful. But after a year of nonstop work, I realized something important—yet counterintuitive. Chasing performance alone doesn't create success. But focusing on success first ensures that great performance follows.

At first, I thought my job was to optimize every little process. Make check-in faster, reduce housekeeping times, increase online bookings, respond to guest reviews within 30 minutes.

We were performing well, but something felt off. Despite hitting all these small targets, we weren't growing at the rate I had envisioned. I was so focused on daily execution that I wasn't asking: *Are we actually moving toward long-term success?*

That's when I realized: High performance doesn't always lead to success. But a focus on success always improves performance.

Defining Success First, Then Aligning Performance

Instead of measuring random efficiency metrics, I redefined success and let performance align with the bigger vision.

Success meant:

- Guests who weren't just satisfied but emotionally connected to the brand.
- Employees who weren't just productive but motivated and loyal.
- Revenue that wasn't just stable but consistently growing.

Then, I aligned performance goals to match:

Instead of just speeding up check-in, we improved the entire arrival experience so guests felt welcomed, not rushed.

Instead of just increasing bookings, we focused on attracting repeat guests who became brand ambassadors.

Instead of just reducing costs, we invested in personalized service enhancements that increased guest loyalty.

By shifting the focus from efficiency to impact, we achieved both great performance and lasting success.

The Turning Point: Changing How We Measured Success

One evening, I sat with my team and asked: "How do we measure success in a way that actually matters?"

Together, we redefined our key success indicators:

Guest Experience Success:

- Not just fast response times, but guest engagement and emotional connection.

- Not just occupancy rates, but repeat bookings and guest referrals.

Employee Success:

- Not just work output, but employee satisfaction and retention.
- Not just productivity metrics, but team collaboration and leadership development.

Financial Success:

- Not just monthly revenue, but long-term profitability and sustainable growth.
- Not just cutting costs, but investing in innovations that improve guest experience.

That shift changed everything.

The Impact: Success Became the Driving Force

Once we started focusing on success first, our performance naturally improved:

Guest loyalty skyrocketed because they felt a deeper emotional connection.

Employee performance increased because they believed in the bigger vision.

Profitability improved because we weren't just chasing short-term efficiency—we were building long-term value.

One day, a guest told me: "I've stayed at many great hotels, but Mirabelle feels different. It doesn't just work well—it feels special." That's when I knew—focusing on success created a lasting impact, not just daily wins.

Final Lesson: Performance Is the Result, Not the Goal

Great performance alone doesn't guarantee success. Defining success first ensures that performance aligns with the right outcomes. The best businesses don't just optimize daily tasks—they build toward something bigger.

At Mirabelle, we don't just measure performance. We define success, then let performance follow.

Ensure the Feasibility of Your Plan

When I first started Mirabelle, I had a bold vision: Create a boutique hotel that felt personal and deeply connected to the local culture, build a sustainable and socially responsible business model, and expand rapidly to new locations. But I made a critical mistake: I focused on the vision without asking whether the plan was actually feasible. A dream without a clear execution plan is just wishful thinking. I learned the hard way that a plan must be realistic, actionable, and sustainable—otherwise, it won't succeed.

The Reality Check: My First Unfeasible Plan

Early on, I set overly ambitious goals:

- Open two more locations within 18 months.
- Launch a luxury spa and rooftop restaurant.
- Double our revenue in one year.

It looked great on paper.

But when I sat down to evaluate it, I realized we didn't have the financial stability for rapid expansion, our team lacked the expertise to manage new services, and we didn't have the systems to scale operations efficiently. That's when I had my first major leadership lesson: A great idea means nothing if it can't be executed. Instead of chasing an impossible dream, I needed to adjust my plan to something achievable.

How I Ensured Feasibility: The Three-Step Process

I developed a three-step process to test the feasibility of any plan before committing to it.

Step 1: Conduct a Reality Check

Does my plan match our current capabilities?

Do we have the right resources, finances, and team?

What risks could prevent success?

Reality Check Example:

Instead of opening two new locations at once, I adjusted my plan to open one location within three years—ensuring we had the right foundation first.

Step 2: Run the Numbers

Does this plan make financial sense?

Do I have a clear cost-benefit analysis?

What's the break-even point?

Financial Example:

For our expansion, I calculated that opening a second location required $500,000, but we only had $200,000 in capital.

Instead of taking a risky loan, we secured a strategic partnership to co-fund the expansion—avoiding excessive financial strain.

Step 3: Test the Plan Before Scaling

Can we implement a small version of this plan first?

What early indicators will tell us if it's working?

Can we adjust quickly if things don't go as expected?

Testing Example:

Before launching a full luxury spa, we tested limited wellness offerings (yoga classes, in-room massages). This allowed us to measure guest interest, adjust pricing based on demand, see if it aligned with our brand.

By testing first, we avoided major financial risks and validated demand before making a big investment.

The Turning Point: Feasibility Transformed Mirabelle

Once we tested every plan for feasibility, things changed. We made smarter, sustainable growth decisions, we avoided expensive mistakes, and we built confidence in our success plans.

One of my investors told me: "Maya, what makes Mirabelle successful isn't just your vision—it's that you know how to turn vision into reality." That's when I knew—the best ideas are the ones you can actually execute.

Final Lesson: Success Is Built on What's Achievable

Ambition is great, but feasibility turns ambition into success. Every plan should be tested against reality, finances, and execution ability. The smartest leaders don't just dream big—they make sure their dreams can work.

At Mirabelle, we don't chase impossible ideas. We make great ideas happen—because we ensure that they're feasible first.

Ensure that Your Plan Is Risk-tested

When I first started Mirabelle, I believed that if I had a strong business plan and a great team, success would follow. But then, reality hit. Unexpected events—a supplier failure, a sudden drop in bookings, a shortage of employees—tested my business in ways I never anticipated.

That's when I learned: A plan isn't truly strong unless it has been tested for risks. I needed to prepare for the unexpected—because in business, it's not about *if* problems will arise, but *when.*

The Wake-Up Call: The Overbooking Crisis

One summer, Mirabelle was fully booked for a major city event. It was supposed to be a perfect weekend—until I got a frantic call from the front desk. A technical error had overbooked five rooms. Guests were arriving with nowhere to stay. We had no immediate backup plan. It was a disaster. I had to personally apologize to guests, pay for alternative accommodations, and deal with angry reviews. That night, I realized I had a great business plan, but it wasn't risk-tested. I vowed never to let this happen again.

Learning from the Best: How Risk Management Works

I started studying how top businesses approach risk management and discovered five key principles that professional organizations use:

Identify Potential Risks Before They Happen

Successful businesses don't wait for disasters—they anticipate them. They maintain a comprehensive risk register that includes every possible threat, from financial risks to cybersecurity breaches.

At Mirabelle, we identified:

- Overbooking errors
- Supplier failures
- Market downturns
- Negative PR crises
- Technology failures

Prevent Risks Proactively

Instead of waiting for problems, put safeguards in place. If something could go wrong, there must be a preventive measure in place.

At Mirabelle, we:

- Introduced an automatic real-time booking system.
- Built strong relationships with backup suppliers.
- Trained employees on PR crisis response.

Minimize Residual Risks

Some risks can't be eliminated completely, but their impact can be reduced. For example, fire drills won't prevent a fire but will reduce damage and save lives.

At Mirabelle, we minimized risks by:

- Keeping an emergency fund for unexpected disruptions.
- Offering flexible cancelation policies to keep bookings stable.
- Implementing cybersecurity measures to protect guest data.

Be Ready for Emergencies and Crises

Even the best-prepared companies face unexpected crises. The difference between survival and failure is having a response plan ready.

At Mirabelle, we developed:

- A detailed crisis communication plan for public relations emergencies.
- Emergency procedures for IT failures or power outages.
- A guest service protocol for handling major issues with empathy.

Ensure Business Continuity

A crisis should not bring your business to a halt. Businesses with strong business continuity management recover faster.

At Mirabelle:

- We built a network of partner hotels to relocate guests in case of overbooking, trained employees to take over key roles if a team member was absent, and diversified revenue streams to reduce dependency on seasonal bookings.

Putting Risk-Testing into Action

After learning these principles, I applied them to Mirabelle.

Scenario Testing: Before launching a new booking system, we ran stress tests to simulate real-world peak demand.

Emergency Simulations: We ran drills to see how employees would handle a sudden IT failure.

Financial Risk Assessment: We identified our financial weak points and built a stronger budget buffer.

These steps transformed how we handled risk at Mirabelle.

The Impact: How Risk-Testing Strengthened Mirabelle

Once we started risk-testing every plan, we saw huge improvements: We handled crises with confidence instead of panic, we prevented costly mistakes before they happened, and our reputation improved because we were always prepared.

One day, a guest told me: "I've stayed at many hotels, but Mirabelle always feels like everything runs smoothly—even when challenges come up." That's when I knew—risk-tested plans don't just protect a business; they make it stronger.

Final Lesson: A Plan That Can't Handle Risks Isn't a Good Plan

Success isn't just about having a great plan. It's about preparing for what could go wrong.

The best businesses don't just react to problems, they prevent them. Every plan should be tested for risks before it's implemented.

At Mirabelle, we don't just plan for success. We prepare for everything that could go wrong, so that when challenges come, we don't survive—we thrive.

Be Flexible and Agile in Your Planning

When I first launched Mirabelle, I believed in having a solid plan and sticking to it, but reality had other ideas: unexpected market changes, shifting guest expectations, and operational surprises. No matter how perfect my plan seemed, the world around me was constantly changing. That's when I realized: Success isn't about following a rigid plan—it's about adapting quickly when things change.

The Lesson: The Pandemic Shock

Like many businesses, Mirabelle was thriving—until the pandemic hit. Almost overnight, cancelations flooded in, tourism came to a halt, revenue dropped dramatically. At first, I panicked. My original business plan hadn't accounted for this. Then I asked myself: *What if the businesses that survive aren't the ones with the best plans—but the ones that can change plans the fastest?* That's when I embraced flexibility and agility—not as a crisis response, but as a core business strength.

How I Learned to Adapt Quickly

I realized that rigid planning was a liability—so I developed a new three-part approach to agility:

Step 1: Use an Early Warning System:

What trends are shifting?

What are guests and competitors doing differently?

What external factors could impact my business?

Example: The businesses that survived COVID-19 best weren't the ones who reacted late, but those who saw it coming early and adjusted.

Before travel stopped completely, I noticed other industries shifting to remote work. I launched long-term extended-stay options for remote workers before the market caught on. By the time competitors started adjusting, we were already fully booked with professionals seeking quiet workspaces.

Lesson: Agility isn't just about reacting to change. It's about detecting change before it happens.

Step 2: Plan for Multiple Scenarios

What if demand spikes unexpectedly?

What if suppliers can't deliver on time?

What if regulations shift overnight?

Example: Instead of assuming one fixed path, I prepared three different plans:

1. Best Case: Travel demand rebounds quickly → Prepare for an influx of guests.
2. Worst Case: Travel stays limited → Focus on local markets, staycations, and private workspace rentals.
3. Regulatory Shock: New government restrictions limit operations → Move more services online (e.g., virtual concierge, digital events).

Lesson: Businesses that have multiple plans in place adjust faster than those who scramble last-minute.

Step 3: Build a Culture of Agility

Can my team adjust quickly?

Are employees empowered to make decisions?

Do we have contingency plans for different scenarios?

Example: Instead of slow, top-down decisions, we:

- Empowered employees to suggest real-time improvements.
- Tested small-scale changes before committing long-term.
- Held monthly "Adapt and Innovate" meetings to brainstorm new ideas.

One of our best pivots?

A front desk employee suggested a mobile check-in system to reduce physical contact during COVID-19. We tested it within a week. Guests loved it. We made it permanent—even post-pandemic.

Lesson: Agility isn't just about leadership decisions. It's about empowering your entire team to adapt.

The Competitive Advantage of Agility

While many hotels struggled to stay open, Mirabelle was growing and thriving. We created new revenue streams, we adjusted operations to meet evolving guest needs, and we built a team culture focused on innovation.

One guest, a startup founder, told me: "The reason I love staying at Mirabelle is because it feels like a living, evolving space—not a hotel stuck in outdated routines." That's when I knew: Being agile wasn't just about survival; it was about long-term success and competitive advantage.

Final Lesson: Plan to Adapt, Not Just to Execute

A rigid plan is a fragile plan. Businesses that survive are the ones that adapt the fastest.

Agility isn't just about reacting—it's about proactively anticipating change.

At Mirabelle, we don't just make plans, we stay flexible, we embrace change, and we evolve constantly—so that no matter what happens, we're always ready.

Chapter Four

Pursue Practical Implementation (STEP 4)

Within many industries, implementation of plans is often the biggest challenge toward success. With the KAIZUNO method, clear processes, measurable goals, inspiring leadership, a supportive culture, and the right tools help you work efficiently toward sustainable success.

"Implementation is the only way to success."

—Thomas Edison

Be a Competent Team that Enjoys Working Together

People and teams are the driving forces behind every success. A strong team combines all the essential competencies necessary for successful implementation. Professional skills, experience, and diverse perspectives complement each other, enabling challenges to be overcome together. Good coordination and targeted use of each individual's strengths ensure that teams remain high-performing.

Good organizations value not only their employees. They understand that they can substantially increase the performance of their organization if they create good teams from good people. Guided by inspiring leadership, a team of 5 people performs much better than 5 individual people with the same set of talents.

Role model leaders create and sustain good teams by:

- bringing together diverse skill sets of individual people with experience in different disciplines.
- promoting regular team-building activities to strengthen cooperation and trust.
- offering training and further education to continuously expand team knowledge.
- agreeing clear roles and responsibilities to maximize the efficiency of teamwork.
- using regular feedback sessions to reflect and continuously improve team performance.

- encouraging an open communication culture within teams and across different teams.
- recognizing and rewarding the contributions of each team member to increase motivation and commitment.

Good practice examples:

Airbus

- Brings together teams from different countries and disciplines to work on complex aerospace projects.
- Collaboration between engineers, scientists and business professionals ensures diverse perspectives and innovative solutions.
- Promotes cross-team collaboration through shared digital platforms and regular meetings.
- Their "teamwork spirit" initiative encourages collaboration across departments and countries.
- They invest heavily in employee training programs and recognize team efforts through internal awards like the Airbus Innovation Awards.

IKEA

- Teams are built with diversity in mind, ensuring a mix of skills, cultures, and experiences to solve complex challenges.
- Team collaboration is part of IKEA's core values, fostering a culture of "togetherness".
- They host regular workshops and fun events to strengthen bonds between team members.
- They celebrate teams' contributions through awards and internal promotions to maintain motivation and commitment.

Secure Support of Strong Partners and Suppliers

No organization can do everything alone. Strong partners and reliable suppliers complement missing competencies, secure resources and contribute valuable know-how. Partners are key to organizational success. They provide critical support that cannot be covered internally, while suppliers ensure a smooth supply of materials and services.

Good collaboration with partners and suppliers requires that you provide a solid and strong basis for cooperation. This requires common goals, clear win-win agreements that benefit both sides, mutual trust and reliability. The more attractive you are as an organization to third parties, the better partners and suppliers will work with you.

You can ensure sustainable win-win relationships with your partners and suppliers by:

- agreeing clear targets and mutual expectations to avoid misunderstanding.
- working transparently and fairly together to promote trust and long-term cooperation.
- carefully coordinating work with your partners and suppliers to ensure mutual benefit.
- regularly evaluating partner performance to continuously optimize collaboration.
- helping your partners and suppliers to improve their performance and compliance with sustainability expectations from social interest partners.
- promoting knowledge exchange and best practice to grow together.
- exchanging open and honest feedback to continuously improve cooperation.

Good practice examples:

BMW Group

- Integrates sustainability into its supplier relationships by requiring environmental standards and monitoring suppliers' CO_2 footprints.

- Collaborates with suppliers to adopt renewable energy and reduce emissions, aligning with its long-term sustainability goals.

- Ensures that all partners understand their role in meeting shared targets through clear contracts and regular performance evaluations.

Siemens

- Collaborates with partners and suppliers to integrate advanced technologies such as IoT and AI into manufacturing processes, improving efficiency and sustainability.

- Helps suppliers implement Industry 4.0 technologies, enabling smart production processes and energy optimization.

- Valuates supplier performance through its Supplier Relationship Management system, ensuring continuous improvement and compliance with environmental and ethical standards.

Maintain a Supportive Leadership

Good leadership provides orientation, makes clear decisions, and ensures stability—even in challenging times. It creates trust by acting reliably and setting comprehensible priorities. Important characteristics are open and appreciative communication as well as the ability to identify problems early and actively solve them.

In crisis situations, good leadership remains capable of action and makes conscious decisions to guide employees and teams safely through uncertainties. Supportive leadership strengthens the self-responsibility of employees and teams, and enables them to actively grow.

"Take care of your employees, and they will take care of your business."

—Richard Branson, Entrepreneur

Good leadership is a key success factor of any organization in all phases that create success:

STEP 1 (Strive for success)

Leaders define the purpose of the organization, inspire a positive attitude of employees and teams und use their strengths, ensure everyone is in harmony with the identity of the organization and agree on an attractive target image.

STEP 2 (Thrive through relationships)

Leaders involve success-related interest groups, manage and maintain relations, understand their current and future expectations and create a balanced expectation image as a solid and robust fundament for the plan.

STEP 3 (Embrace balanced planning)

Leaders have good answers to all expectations, know how they can achieve success with a good plan, define suitable success goals, balance success with performance and ensure the plan is feasible, risk-tested and flexible.

STEP 4 (Pursue practical implementation)

Leaders sustain a supportive culture to ensure teams enjoy working together, direct value creation with attractive products and services, support the use of relevant data and knowledge transfer, select helpful technologies, supervise operational risk management and are role models for sustainability.

STEP 5 (Secure sustainable success)

Leaders analyze feedback from interest groups and select the best ways to increase their satisfaction, harvest and communicate the fruits of success with all relevant interest groups and are responsible to secure the future.

What Makes a Good Leader?

Leadership is like conducting an orchestra, where each individual contributes an important part to the harmony of the whole. Good leadership means not only defining and communicating clear goals, but also to create an atmosphere of trust and cooperation. In such an environment, everyone feels seen, valued, and motivated to give their best.

Good leaders do not act as autocratic bosses, but as inspiring mentors who recognize and promote the strengths of each employee and team, create space for innovation, support personal growth and encourage everyone to think outside the box. In this way, leaders not only create joint success, but also a working culture based on respect, appreciation and common goals.

These are 5 characteristics of truly outstanding leadership:

1. *Adaptability in the face of uncertainty*: Role model leaders can not only act in predefined scenarios, but will lead the way in the midst of ambiguity and uncertainty. They are not overwhelmed by uncertainty but rather use those moments as opportunities for reorientation and innovation.

2. *Intuitive foresight:* Beyond the usual planning activities, outstanding leaders have an almost intuitive ability to anticipate

future trends and developments. This foresight allows them to decide proactive plans and direct their quick and effective implementation to create competitive advantage.

3. *Empathetic conflict resolution*: An outstanding leader recognizes conflicts very early and resolves them with deep empathy, by understanding all the individual parties involved. This ability reduces the risk of negative impact considerably.

4. *Silent resilience:* Role model leaders are charismatic people who also demonstrate a quiet, unobtrusive resilience at the same time. In moments of pressure or crisis, they radiate a calm confidence that gives their employees and teams stability and hope, without any fuss or theatrical gestures.

5. *Encouraging initiative*: Instead of control and micromanagement, outstanding leaders encourage their teams to take initiative in a self-responsible role. This creates a climate in which everyone feels encouraged to think and act independently. Mistakes are understood as opportunities for learning and growth rather than failures.

Treat Each Other Well

In teams, treating each other well makes a huge difference. Those who feel comfortable in the team are respected, and enjoy coming to work to give their best. An appreciative culture ensures cohesion, efficiency, and motivation—and also makes the organization attractive as an employer on the labor market to skilled professionals. When everyone supports and can rely on each other, work becomes more enjoyable, more meaningful and more successful.

In any organization, leaders are responsible for shaping a culture in which all employees feel inspired, valued, encouraged, recognized and supported—every day, in good and in bad times. Workplace culture, shaped by leaders at all levels, is more powerful than any strategy or plan in driving employee engagement, motivation and long-term success.

"Culture eats strategy for breakfast."

—Peter Drucker

What Is a Supportive Corporate Culture and What Is It Worth?

Let's imagine that your family is a small company (e.g., a bakery), in which each person plays a specific role, from carrying out everyday tasks to fixing problems. The way you interact with each other, your values, your humor and your shared memories, that is your "family culture". It shapes you, guides your behavior, and creates a sense of belonging and security for everyone.

The same principles apply to corporate culture, since they are natural and therefore universally valid. Like in a family, corporate culture consists of a set of written and unwritten rules, values and behaviors that guide all actions and decisions in the workplace. It is the invisible glue that holds everything together. Just like in a family, it is important that organizations create and maintain a culture that is healthy for everyone and therefore leads to success.

The behaviors that support the success of your organization in the best possible way depend a lot on your identity and your purpose. A tax authority will need different behaviors than a marketing agency.

But what is this corporate culture really worth?

It is worth more than you might realize at first glance. A positive corporate culture promotes a high level of employee satisfaction and loyalty. It can help you attract and retain the best talents because people enjoy working in a place where they feel valued, appreciated and supported. This is a critical success factor, especially in times of skills shortages.

A supportive corporate culture also increases your productivity by creating conditions that support creativity and innovation. If everyone follows the same basic principles and no one has to constantly reassure themselves, everyone can work faster and more efficiently as less time is spent on misunderstandings and pointless conflicts.

Promoting a positive corporate culture should therefore not be a by-product or a loveless "change workshop", but a conscious and continuous investment by the leadership team.

In a nutshell, good culture:

- Has a strong and resilient fundament of values with leaders as role models
- Promotes open feedback, values mutual appreciation and cherishes mindfulness
- Supports open and transparent communication to strengthen trust and cooperation
- Increases motivation and commitment by rewards and celebrates success
- Values diversity and inclusion and appreciates different perspectives and ideas
- Promotes sustainability and innovation
- Supports flexible working models to improve the work-life balance
- Supports individuals and teams to collaborate everywhere.

Ensure Good Process Management

Processes are there to transfer the plan into everyday working life. This turns plans into products and services that are attractive to your customers. Process management ensures that all processes in your organization work together in a harmonious way like an orchestra. In a symphony orchestra, good process management creates a fantastic listening experience for the guests. This is another word for success.

In the same way, good process management in your organization ensures that your customers are delighted. In the orchestra, the overarching process manager is the conductor. In your organization, the process managers are your leaders.

What Are Processes?

Almost everything you do repetitively every day in your private life is a process: brushing your teeth, commuting to work, working, sport in the gym, and even preparing dinner.

There are basically two different types of processes:

Value-adding processes: These add value to customers.

Supporting processes: These support the value-adding processes to further increase their value.

If "value-adding" in your private life is earning money, then "working" is the only value-adding process of the 5 process examples above. All other processes support this value-adding process, since they all make sure that you are able and healthy enough to work. The same rule applies to organizations.

Value-adding Processes

Typical value-adding processes are:

Designing, making, and delivering your products and services. This includes sourcing all material and services to do that (supply chain).

Managing relationships with your interest groups. This includes understanding expectations, marketing, sales and care of customers.

Value-Adding Processes, Simplified

For a small bakery, the value creation processes could be:

1. Winning customer orders

The bakery offers a range of freshly baked, fragrant bread rolls and other baked goods in line with customer expectations. It advertises the fact that its bread is fresher and the selection is larger than at other bakeries.

2. Carrying out customer orders

This includes the purchase of the ingredients and the actual baking process. Customer expectations regarding quality and regional sourcing are taken into account.

3. Completing customer orders

This includes the appealing presentation of baked goods in the shop and the sales process. Positive (e.g., a smile) or negative feedback is quickly collected before customers leave the shop.

> ***"Breakfast preparation, breakfast execution and breakfast control. Take this order and replace the word breakfast with your topic."***
>
> —Prof. Bühner, University of Passau

Supporting Processes

Typical supporting processes include the management of people and talents, finances, quality, compliance risks, environment, health, safety, IT and digitalization, administration, and infrastructure. Process management is also a supporting process.

Supporting Processes, Simplified

For a small bakery, the major supporting processes could be:

1. Employee training

The owner ensures that all employees are well-trained and highly motivated. Training of salespeople includes friendly behavior toward customers, even in critical situations.

2. Furnace maintenance

Regular maintenance by the baker is supported by a professional maintenance service, which is commissioned on a variable basis depending on requirements.

3. Cleaning

Proper cleaning ensures that every surface shines and every corner is hygienic, creating a welcoming atmosphere for customers and a safe working environment for employees.

Process Ownership and Accountability

Since processes are the backbone of any organization, every process needs a dedicated owner. Process owners should be experienced, competent, and capable managers who are fully accountable and responsible for their process regarding:

- definition and communication
- usability and correct execution (process adherence)

- target setting
- performance measurements against targets
- interfaces with other processes
- digitalization
- qualification of process users
- operational risk management
- process improvements

Process ownership is a very challenging leadership task that is quite underestimated by most organizations.

Process Definition and Graphic Visualization

Process owners define—in alignment with other relevant process owners, specifically at process interfaces—their processes as an interconnected, harmonious network in a way that it delivers expected results with a defined performance—like clockwork.

This process definition includes:

- a detailed description
- all relevant interfaces with other processes
- all related responsibilities of process users
- all relevant inputs and outputs
- descriptions of all related digital systems including all interfaces
- descriptions of all other relevant resources, e.g., AI support
- links to all relevant procedures and work instructions
- all relevant process performance indicators
- related performance targets, as derived from success goals
- external performance benchmarks, if available

Process flowcharts are a fundamental method to visualize processes, defined by process owners for process users. They provide two basic dimensions of information about processes in a 2-dimensional chart.

The sequence of process steps and decision points, interfaces to other processes and links to related work instructions, digital systems and performance indicators, roles and responsibilities for every single process step.

Organizing flowcharts according to roles and responsibilities of process users, line by line, creates horizontal "swimlanes" for each process role. The process "flows through different swimlanes". Regardless of digital mapping tools, this graphical swimlane methodology is probably the easiest way for process owners to document, communicate, and explain their process to users.

Swimlanes make it easy to identify inefficiencies, redundancies, and areas for improvement within a process, and at interfaces. Many years of the authors' experience confirm that users understand process documentation on the basis of graphical swimlanes much easier than any other way of documentation.

Why Is Process Performance So Important?

Your customers don't care about your organization's processes, they just care about their satisfaction with your products and services—which are the results of your processes.

We argued earlier: "Focus on success, then on performance"; a good plan has the most direct influence on your success. But then, good process performance also supports your success. It increases the efficiency of your value-adding and supporting processes. This is a competitive success factor for your organization.

In your private life, you instinctively measure the performance of your processes every day. You compare measurements with targets and improve these processes to achieve your targets. Here are some examples from daily life:

To save time brushing your teeth, you might improve your brushing technique or buy an electric toothbrush.

To save energy on your daily commute to work, you might change the way of transport (e.g., from car to bus or bike) to optimize travel time and reduce your CO_2 footprint.

To optimize quality and cost of grocery shopping, you might select better shops, optimize your way of shopping, or change your diet.

To improve time and quality of homework, children may change their way of working.

To save time for dinner preparation, you may buy a cutting machine for vegetables.

Measuring Process Performance

Process owners define—in alignment with other relevant process owners, specifically at process interfaces—process performance indicators (PIs) in all relevant dimensions, including the classic three ones: quality, time, and cost.

Performance indicators with high impact on success are called Key Performance Indicators (KPIs). An example could be the delivery time for products, since this time has a direct influence on customer satisfaction.

Note: The authors found many organizations who use the term "KPI" for all kinds of performance measurements, important ones and not important ones. This is wrong. In line with common sense, most process performance indicators are PIs, and only some of them are KPIs, since they are key to success.

Some organizations even use "KPIs" to address measurements of success. This is fundamentally wrong. Success is measured with a completely different set of indicators, since success is the result of process performance, not performance per se. An example could be the measurement of customer satisfaction (STEP 5) by net promoter score. A high net promotor score is the result of high-performing processes.

Examples of process performance indicators in organizations are on-time delivery rate, first-pass yield or compliance rate. The specific quantitative measures of performance indicators are defined by underlying metrics, which provide detailed numerical data on key aspects of process performance. Examples could be cost per transaction, numbers of errors per unit or percentage of capacity used.

Since the one and only reason for measuring process performance is the desire to improve processes, all process performance indicators need to be defined in a SMART way: Specific, Measurable, Actionable, Relevant and measured over Time. Without measuring process performance, processes cannot be improved.

Process Performance Targets

Why do you need to define performance targets? Without performance targets, any process performance is fine: if you buy groceries and you don't set performance targets regarding quality and price for your shopping process, you buy good and bad quality, as well as cheap and expensive items. Only if you define quality and price targets, you will buy those groceries that you really want.

As you deploy your plan into the operational world of processes, you need to translate your success goals into process performance targets in a balanced way: all process performance targets together must deliver and support the totality of the success goals.

If you adjust your success goals—for instance due to a critical change in expectations of interest groups—you have to adjust all relevant process performance targets accordingly.

If you track process performance indicators over time against performance targets, you can discover trends. If you ensure (e.g., by software) that you get a system alert if a target is not achieved, this alert can trigger data-driven decisions of your process owners. They can then improve the related process to ensure target achievement.

Graphical visualization allows process owners and even users to identify performance problems in good time so that they can react with countermeasures before the problem has a negative impact on success.

Additionally, you can compare critical process performance targets with external benchmarks, e.g., process performance from competitors, if available. These comparisons can provide additional indications how to improve your critical processes, to ensure your competitiveness.

Some organizations use software-supported graphical "performance dashboards" to provide an overview of all important performance indicators compared with relevant targets (and benchmarks). Color codes determined by intelligent digital tools can indicate critical trends and trigger alarms, to allow timely and prompt intervention by process owners. These dashboards are a dynamic, real-time, and state-of-the-art alternative to conventional performance reports—still used by many organizations today—which are outdated as soon as they are published.

Excellent organizations have smart, AI-supported mechanisms in place which analyze performance data patterns in a smart way to simulate future trends. This enables process owners to discover even small target deviations proactively, which in turn allows timely intervention and corrective actions, before interest groups (e.g., customers) are negatively affected.

Good Measuring Instruments for Process Performance

You constantly measure what you do in everyday life: how many kilometers you have driven, how much money you have spent, how many calories you have burned during exercise, how much time you spend to prepare dinner, or how many hours you have spent on screen time.

These measurements become more meaningful if you see them in the context of your success goals. Take, for example, the success goal: "more quality of life". If this means for you to commute less, eat healthier, use fewer resources, keep your body in better shape, and spend less time in the digital world, then you can set performance targets for all these activities and try to achieve them. If you make the right individual improvements, then overall, you will come closer to your success goal—"more quality of life".

Instruments for measuring process performance must fit the process. Wrong instruments to measure something can lead to inaccurate results and poor decisions. Here are a few examples from daily life:

- Using a bathroom scale to measure very small objects like jewelry—too imprecise for small weights.

- Estimating tire pressure by looking at the tire instead of using a pressure gauge—visual checks don't reliably reveal under-inflation.

- Measuring employee performance by hours worked instead of productivity or quality of output—long hours don't always mean good work.

- Using customer complaint numbers to measure overall satisfaction—doesn't account for silent, unhappy customers who just leave.

- Using the number of likes on social media to measure personal success—popularity doesn't always reflect true achievement.

In modern organizations, digitalization keeps making many measurements considerably easier. If a modern production facility is equipped with Industry 4.0, for example, digital measurements take place directly in the production system and are forwarded automatically to a digital dashboard.

Process Improvements

To ensure effective process improvements, good organizations have standard improvement procedures in place, e.g., on the basis of proven philosophies like KAIZEN or PDCA (Plan-Do-Check-Act). Process improvement activities are typically directed by process owners, who wisely involve process users in improvement activities. They have the deepest knowledge of the process they execute every day.

Since any changes of success plans will have to be implemented on an operational process level, the relevant processes must also be changed accordingly. This means that all processes need to be flexible and agile—easy to change.

You may argue that by definition, processes are structured, so they are rigid and cannot be changed easily. Here is the requirement for successful organizations: define your processes in a way that they are structured AND agile at the same time. This is not a contradiction. Structured does not mean rigid. Excellent organizations find the right balance between structure and agility.

A great example of a process that is structured and agile is the Toyota Production System (TPS); specifically, its Just-in-Time (JIT) manufacturing process.

Structured: Toyota follows a highly standardized production process with clear workflows, quality checks, and efficiency principles (e.g., lean manufacturing, Kanban, Kaizen). Every worker knows their role and there are precise procedures to ensure quality and minimal waste.

Agile: Despite being structured, TPS is highly adaptable to changes in demand, supply chain disruptions, and customer preferences. The Kanban system allows production to adjust quickly based on real-time needs. Kaizen (continuous improvement) ensures that employees can suggest process changes, allowing the system to evolve without disrupting its core structure.

Example in Action: If demand for a certain car model suddenly increases, Toyota can quickly scale production up without breaking the structured workflow. If a supplier issue occurs, the system reallocates resources while keeping production efficient. During the COVID-19 pandemic, Toyota rapidly shifted production to prioritize essential vehicles while maintaining quality and efficiency.

Comparing or benchmarking processes with competitors, industry standards and good or best practices is a powerful approach to ensure competitiveness. But be aware that most benchmarks cannot simply be copied/pasted into your organization. Rather, benchmarks require intelligent adaptation to your individual situation. There are cases where organizations blindly copied/pasted benchmarks and lost business.

Intelligent benchmarking is a key leadership task and should not be outsourced to a partner who is not fully aware of the organization's identity and success goals. Here is an example where stupid benchmarking caused substantial damage to an organization:

The New Coke Disaster

In the early 80s, Coca-Cola saw that Pepsi was gaining market share, partly due to its "Pepsi Challenge" taste tests. In 1985, Coca-Cola introduced "New Coke", a sweeter version of its original formula, aiming to better compete with Pepsi. There was a massive consumer backlash, and Coca-Cola had to bring back the original formula as "Coca-Cola Classic" just 79 days after the "New Coke" launch. Coca-Cola lost millions in production and marketing costs. Their reputation took a hit, as people saw them as abandoning their legacy.

Measure Progress of Improvement Activities

If process improvements have been identified, they have to be implemented. Process improvements can be classified according to their importance and impact, and the amount of time, people, and resources they consume.

Most organizations implement small process improvement "activities" typically within a few weeks. Those activities can be handled with simple activity management instruments that all organizations use. Examples are:

Kanban board: simple board with columns (e.g., to-do, in progress, done) that visually tracks work. This helps teams to quickly improve their workflow.

PDCA cycle: Plan (identify an issue and possible solution); Do (implement an improvement); Check (measure the results of the change); Act (standardize if successful or adjust if needed).

Ask WHY five times: Why was the order delayed? → The supplier was late. Why was the supplier late? → They didn't receive the request on time. Why? → The request was stuck in processing. Why? → The system flagged it for approval. Why? → The approval process is manual. Solution? Automate approvals for standard orders.

Larger process improvements are usually managed as projects. Mature organizations have "project management" approaches in place to ensure that large process improvements are managed in professional ways.

Here are some basic principles of project management:

Clear goals and planning—every project needs clear success goals and a step-by-step plan to reach them.

Roles and responsibilities—everyone in the project should know their job and who is responsible for what to avoid confusion and delays.

Time and budget management—projects need milestones with deliverables, deadlines, and budgets.

Communication and teamwork—good projects need strong teamwork and clear communication.

Tracking progress and adapting—things don't always go as planned, so it's important to check progress regularly and make adjustments if needed to reach the goal.

Process Adherence

Process users are supposed to execute processes exactly in the way they are defined. If users deviate from the plan, process performance and outcomes may change. This is why process owners need to check "process adherence" from time to time.

Nobody knows processes better than users, who live their processes every day. This is why creative process users often find ways to improve their processes as they use them. This means that there are two versions of the same process available: the original one that was released by the process owner, and the adapted one with different performance and results.

To professionally consider improvement suggestions from process users, they discuss the idea with the responsible process owner. Owner and users agree on a regular process improvement, which will change the process definition and create a new process version.

Example:

"Fast Burger Trick"—A Process Shortcut Gone Wrong

Employees of a well-known fast-food chain are trained to follow a strict process to ensure that every burger is cooked and assembled to meet quality and safety standards. In some locations, employees wanted to speed up service times (to improve customer satisfaction and meet internal performance targets). Instead of cooking burgers fresh to order, some employees pre-made large batches of burgers and kept them wrapped under heat lamps for longer than allowed.

What went wrong? The burgers were no longer fresh, leading to customer complaints. Holding food too long reduced quality, making the brand look bad. In some cases, food safety was compromised when burgers sat out too long. The fast-food chain had to reinforce training and increase checks to ensure that employees followed the correct process.

Provide Attractive Products and Services

Products and services are the result of value-adding processes. Both products and services require a complete supply chain. Many organizations offer products and services at the same time, e.g., a car dealership sells cars but also carries out regular servicing for these vehicles. However, there are also pure product companies (e.g., manufacturers of windshield wiper blades) or pure service providers (e.g., driving schools).

Products

These are tangible or intangible results of value-adding processes, e.g., baked rolls or a software product. The production of products requires a complete and reliable supply chain that ensures that production, quality, and availability are guaranteed at all times—e.g., the reliable procurement of flour for the bread rolls.

A good product not only meets expectations but delights customers. It is functional, reliable, and appealing—while being economical to produce. Regular lifecycle development keeps products relevant and competitive. Those who recognize market changes early and respond to them stay ahead.

Products are increasingly manufactured by automated systems (e.g., baked rolls in large bakeries) and robots (e.g., the body shell of cars made of steel and aluminum). Humans tend to take on more monitoring and maintenance tasks. Regardless of the level of automation, production must always be perfectly synchronized with the supply chain—if the flour is missing, no bread rolls can be baked.

Services

These are intangible results of value-adding processes, e.g., serving baked rolls in a bakery-café. Similar to products, services also require a supply chain, e.g., the equipment in a bakery-café. As a rule, services also require products.

A good service not only meets expectations but creates a positive experience. It is reliable, professional, and customer-oriented—and can be flexibly adapted to individual needs. Often, services complement products and turn them into a complete solution for customers, whether through consultation, maintenance, or additional services.

Services are also increasingly being automated through digitalization. For example, many schools offer their students prepared learning modules via video, insurance companies put important documents in their portals and automatically inform their customers about updates. This allows organizations to significantly reduce their own costs, while the opposite is true for customers. Customers are taking on more and more tasks that employees used to do. This can create customer dissatisfaction and eventually a negative impact on the success of the service provider.

What Are the Characteristics of Good Products and Services?

Let's imagine a sunny morning when you stroll into your favorite bakery around the corner. The smell of freshly baked bread and the sight of crispy rolls and delicious pastries make our mouth water. But what makes this visit so special?

In the bakery, you experience a harmonious fusion of product and service. The bread, made with artisan craftsmanship and selected ingredients, represents the quality and authenticity that you look for in a good product.

But a good product alone is not enough. Service plays an equally important role in our bakery experience. The friendly bakers, who greet you with a warm smile, are happy to advise you and perhaps even offer you a small piece of cake to try, creating an atmosphere of warmth and welcome.

In the business world, you strive for a similar symbiosis of products and services. You endeavor for a relationship with your customers that goes beyond the mere purchase. To do this, you need to know the expectations and needs of your customers.

"People don't want to buy a drill; they want a hole in the wall to hang a picture."

—Theodore Levitt, American Economist
(adapted)

Customers don't actually want products and services but good answers to problems or needs. They buy products and services if they believe that they are a solution for them. To create sustainable value with good products and services, organizations should:

- design the value of their products and services over the complete lifecycle to create an attractive portfolio of value propositions for customers.

- use their competitive advantage and involve key interest groups, market research, networking and influencers during the design phase.

- communicate and sell the value propositions of their products and services to existing and potential customers in convincing ways.

- produce and deliver their products and services in line with the value propositions with the intention to provide maximum benefit for their customers.

Use Suitable Instruments That Fit Your Organization and Goals

A balanced set of suitable management instruments supports processes in further increasing their value for interest groups—just like experienced musicians in a well-conducted orchestra enhance the listening pleasure for the audience with their valuable musical instruments.

Important instruments for organizations are structure, project management, handling of data and information, utilization of knowledge, appropriate documentation, use of technologies, and dealing with risks in everyday life.

Which specific instruments are needed and to what extent depends on the purpose and situation of the organization. A sailboat on Lake Constance needs completely different instruments than a cruise ship on the Atlantic.

Make Your Life Easier with Good Organization

A tidy and well-organized lifestyle helps make life easier and avoid problems. The organizational structure supports the value creation of processes. As processes flow through the organization, the value streams should be optimally guided as in a riverbed.

Good organizational structures make many things easier. Unfortunately, too many current organizational structures have the opposite effect, since they are not aligned with the process world. Ideally, processes and the organizational structure support each other in a perfect way, like two sides of the same coin.

A Good Organizational Structure:

Supports the processes perfectly: A well-designed organizational structure aligns all key functions with processes, in line with the organization's success goals. The role of organizational functions is to support processes in the best possible way.

Provides clear responsibilities and accountabilities: Functional leaders are process owners. Hierarchies and reporting relationships ensure accountability for all important processes, tasks and objectives, streamlining decision-making and execution of plans.

Ensures efficient resource allocation: A sound organizational structure facilitates optimal allocation of people and talents and resources, ensuring processes are well aligned with high-level priorities.

Improves communication and collaboration: Clear communication channels and cross-functional linkages embedded in the organizational structure enhance collaboration across organizational functions, enabling and supporting process performance.

Supports agility and change: Any process changes can be quickly and effectively supported by a flexible organizational structure. This enables the organization to respond quickly and effectively to changes in interest group needs or risks.

A good practice example of aligning processes and organizational structure is the Toyota Production System (TPS).

Toyota ensures that processes drive the organizational structure rather than the other way around. Its structure is designed around value streams rather than traditional hierarchical silos, and teams are organized by processes. The company's focus on lean manufacturing ensures that processes flow smoothly with minimal waste. Organizational roles are clearly defined to support these lean processes, allowing seamless communication and execution.

Employees are not only trained to execute processes, but also encouraged to improve them, creating a culture of inclusion, participation, and innovation. Misalignment between organizational structure and processes can hinder an organization's ability to adapt to industry changes, ultimately impacting its success.

A leading tire manufacturer in the 1970s, with a strong, centralized organizational structure and deeply ingrained processes, focused on producing traditional bias-ply tires. The introduction of radial tire technology required a shift in manufacturing processes and organizational adaptation. However, the company's existing structure and processes were not aligned to accommodate this innovation. The misalignment led to production inefficiencies, quality control issues, and a significant loss in market share as competitors who adapted more effectively to the new technology surpassed the manufacturer.

Be Efficient with Good Project Management

While processes are ongoing, repetitive workflows designed to achieve success by implementing a plan, projects are temporary efforts with a specific goal and defined start and end points. Most organizations use projects to manage improvements on low (process) or high (strategic initiative) level. However, there are several organizations that sell projects to their customers, rather than traditional products or services. Here are some examples:

Siemens Energy designs and builds large energy projects, such as gas-fired or wind power plants tailored to the needs of their customers. SAP delivers enterprise software solutions, often as custom implementation projects. Hyundai Heavy Industries produces massive container ships and offshore drilling platforms as project-based deliveries. Warner Bros. and Disney treat every movie or series production as a unique project; each Olympic Games is essentially a massive project requiring custom planning and execution.

Whether you run your project as an improvement or a customer project, the basic principles of STEPS 1-5 apply here in an appropriate manner:

STEP 1

Before you start your project, you need to define an attractive target picture that appeals to everyone involved.

STEP 2

Before your planning phase, you should involve all your success-related interest groups of your project and understand their needs and expectations. Then, you analyze the overall situation for potential risks, resolve serious conflicts, and consolidate the picture.

STEP 3

Have good answers to the expectations of your project interest groups, define suitable project success goals and realistic deliverables at milestones on the way. Know how to achieve success and balance project success with project performance. Ensure the feasibility of your project plan and that your plan is risk-tested, and be flexible and agile in your planning.

STEP 4

Ensure that a competent project team is put together, and secure support of strong partners and suppliers. Maintain a supportive leadership and culture in your project. Use good project management instruments and tools. Define clear milestones toward project success. Ensure rigorous checks of planned deliverables at those milestones that go beyond "on time" and "in budget". Recalculate the probability of success at every milestone, and related risks. Make strict decisions to change the project plan if the success goal is in danger, and consider the ultimate decision to cancel the project rather than continuing to invest talents and resources in a hopeless project.

STEP 5

At the end of the project, ensure satisfaction of all related interest groups and harvest the fruits of your project success. This can be the increased performance of a key process or a new order from an excited project customer. Don't forget to use feedback from all interest groups involved to review and refine your project management approach for the next project.

If you have more than one project running at the same time, you should align and coordinate your different projects to optimize people and talents, time, cost, resources and success overall. Examples of good practice approaches for the management of multiple projects are:

Project portfolio management, which organizes all projects into a centralized portfolio to manage priorities, people and talents, resources and risks across multiple projects. This enables strategic alignment by ensuring that all projects contribute to the organization's success goals.

Program management office, which oversees the coordination of multiple related projects and acts as a governance hub. It provides standardized methodologies and good practices, and acts as a communication bridge between leaders of different project teams.

Project management dashboards, which track performance across all projects with consistent indicators and provide transparency, comparisons, and real-time insights into project statuses for better decision-making.

PM@Siemens is an award-winning project management methodology designed to enhance project execution for all kinds of large and complex projects. It has even been used successfully for large nuclear power plants, which are among the most complex customer projects on earth. PM@ Siemens includes a globally recognized training and certification program for project managers and ways to ensure a unique project management culture.

Use Relevant Data and Information

Data is created when you do and measure something. Data is also generated when processes run. Leaders and process owners decide whether and how to measure and use this data. Data is worthless without context. Before they create value, they must be interpreted in context (e.g., temperature of the oven in the bakery).

The Good Use of Data:

Enables informed decision-making: Data analysis enables leaders to make evidence-based decisions, reducing reliance on intuition and minimizing errors that could lead to negative impact.

Improves competitive advantage: Organizations that interpret data effectively can identify trends, customer preferences, and market opportunities faster than competitors, giving them an edge in innovation and responsiveness.

Supports risk mitigation: Smart analyses of risk relevant data provide valuable insights into potential risks and vulnerabilities, enabling organizations to anticipate challenges, mitigate risks, and ensure stability.

Enables operational efficiency: Quick and detailed analysis of complex process-related data can identify opportunities for process improvement and related optimization of resources, costs and overall productivity.

Can detect critical quality issues: A detailed, intelligent correlation analysis of data in complex environments can detect critical quality issues early enough to prevent negative impact on, say, customers.

How Does Data Become Valuable Information?

Context turns data into information, which forms the basis for knowledge. Data and information serve companies to better understand interest groups, make informed decisions, and optimize processes.

For highly automated organizations, the massive amount of data is a particular challenge. Without digital assistance, humans are not able to analyze and convert the vast amount of data from a modern production facility into useful information to make correct decisions, e.g., whether maintenance is necessary or not. Therefore, technologies such as artificial intelligence and machine learning are becoming increasingly important for analysis and processing of big data volumes.

"Information is the currency of the 21ˢᵗ century."

—Barack Obama, US President

Several organizations have created significant competitive advantages through superior management of data and information. Here are a few standout examples:

Amazon's recommendation engine analyzes vast amounts of customer data to provide personalized product recommendations, boosting customer satisfaction and sales. This increases customer experience and operational efficiency.

Netflix uses viewing data and sophisticated algorithms to recommend shows and movies tailored to individual user preferences. This increases customer retention and ensures a strong global market share in streaming services.

Uber uses real-time demand and supply data to implement surge pricing, maximizing profits during peak times. Route optimization is enabled by analyzing traffic and ride patterns. This ensures superior ride availability and cost efficiency.

Apply Own and Others' Knowledge in a Useful Way

Knowledge is a combination of information and experience. Knowledge develops over time and loses value if it is not up-to-date. It is stored in people's heads and increasingly in digital systems. Knowledge is valuable if it is relevant, securely stored, easy to find, meaningfully shared, and used in a targeted way (e.g., best baking recipe for bread rolls).

"Knowledge is Power."

—Francis Bacon

Why Is Knowledge So Valuable?

Knowledge is like good wine—it matures over time. But unlike wine, knowledge loses value if it is not constantly renewed. Knowledge is in our heads and increasingly also in our computers and programs. It is valuable as gold if it is up-to-date, securely stored and easily accessible to everyone in the organization.

More and more knowledge is stored in digital systems; however, not all knowledge in a human brain can be easily transferred to digital systems, because emotions also play a role. One example is cycling: it doesn't work without a sense of balance.

Here are some key principles of knowledge management:

Knowledge capture: Collect, classify, and document knowledge from various sources, including humans (e.g., interest groups), processes, systems, and external insights. Organizations that capture and identify key knowledge for their sector have a competitive advantage.

Knowledge organization: Structure knowledge for easy retrieval. The time to find key knowledge when needed is critical. If you use your own knowledge repositories, consider that people are used to find knowledge via AI tools within seconds, not minutes or hours.

Knowledge-sharing: Facilitate access to knowledge through platforms and tools that your employees or partners can easily handle. Encourage a culture of sharing by promoting open communication and teamwork.

Knowledge updates: The only effective way to keep stored knowledge constantly up-to-date is to oblige users to ensure that the knowledge they use is up-to-date themselves.

Knowledge use: Since AI offers access to an incredible amount of knowledge within seconds, it is tempting to use these repositories as the prime source of knowledge. Knowledge provided by AI is a great source for inspiration, but blindly using this knowledge can be dangerous. Here is an example:

Boeing introduced the 737 MAX aircraft to compete with Airbus's more fuel-efficient models. To save time and money, Boeing reused much of the design and training documentation from its older 737 models. They implemented a new system called MCAS (Maneuvering Characteristics Augmentation System) but failed to fully adapt the training materials and user manuals to account for this major change. Pilots were not adequately trained on MCAS functionality, as it was not clearly documented or explained in the manuals. This lack of adaptation contributed to two fatal crashes. The 737 MAX fleet was grounded globally, costing Boeing billions in financial losses and a significant hit to its reputation.

Knowledge protection: It can be tedious to collect critical information over many years that provides the organization with a competitive edge. Loosing information critical for success can easily cause substantial damage. While you constantly read about cyber-attacks in which key knowledge is stolen, other ways for knowledge loss are less well-known, although they can cause just as much damage. One example is poor leadership.

In the early 2010s, a global leader in mobile phones struggled to adapt to the rise of smartphones. During this decline, key engineers and innovative talent left the company due to a toxic culture marked by poor leadership and a lack of appreciation for innovative ideas. Employees who had the knowledge to develop competitive smartphone technology were either sidelined or left the organization. The organization's critical knowledge walked out the door with its employees. This contributed to its inability to compete in the smartphone era, leading to its sale of the mobile phone division to a world-leading technology company in 2014.

Using AI systems can lead to knowledge loss if your provider uses the information you share for their own training purposes.

"Always ask yourself: Why does the source want me to know this?"

—Richard Heinzer, Tip on Media Literacy

Document Relevant Matters Appropriately

Lean and useful documentation is essential for any organization. It serves as a central source of information and knowledge that provides answers quickly and efficiently. This saves time and avoids mistakes in work processes. Important documentation can include high-level plans and related risk and competitor analyses, and also detailed process instructions and performance indicators. Or a well-structured selection of videos for troubleshooting on the basis of real examples right next to the production machine on a tablet. When everyone contributes to ensuring that documented knowledge is always up-to-date, a living knowledge network emerges that promotes collective learning, innovation capability, quick problem-solving, and related success.

Why Is Good Documentation a Critical Success Factor?

The good use of documentation is critical for success of all organizations. Here's why it's so important:

Process management and improvement: Good documentation provides a baseline for analyzing and improving processes. By reviewing documented workflows and related performance indicators, process owners can identify inefficiencies and implement improvements systematically.

Consistency and standardization: Good documentation provides a clear reference for executing processes uniformly across teams and locations, ensuring process adherence, consistent outputs and reducing variability.

Knowledge retention: Well-maintained documentation preserves organizational knowledge, making it accessible to people and teams, even if key individuals leave the organization.

Training and onboarding: Clear process documentation accelerates the onboarding of new employees by serving as a valuable training resource, reducing learning curves and mistakes.

Compliance and risk management: Good documentation demonstrates adherence to rules, regulations or standards, mitigates risks, and ensures accountability in audits or inspections.

Facilitating communication and collaboration: Good documentation acts as a common language across teams, reducing misunderstandings and improving coordination and collaboration in cross-functional environments.

Customer confidence: Accurate documentation demonstrates professionalism and reliability, fostering trust among customers and other interest groups who rely on the organization's processes.

The type of documentation and the resources used should always be based on the needs of the users. For example, essential maintenance-relevant information on a machine that is used every day should be available directly besides the machine. In order to ensure a low barrier for fast, daily use of the documented knowledge or information, it can make sense to use the good old paper form instead of digital media.

Inadequate or poorly managed documentation can lead to significant challenges for organizations. NASA's Mars Climate Orbiter (1999) was a robotic space probe intended to study Mars' climate and atmosphere. The mission failed due to a critical navigation error stemming from a documentation oversight.

Specifically, there was a mismatch in units: one engineering team used imperial units (pound-seconds), while another used metric units (newton-seconds). This discrepancy was not properly documented or communicated. The spacecraft deviated from its intended trajectory, leading to its disintegration upon entering Mars' atmosphere. The mission's failure resulted in a significant financial loss.

Use Helpful (Future) Technologies

Technologies are tools that improve the value of processes, products, and services. While an electric guitar extends the sound spectrum of a conventional guitar, the e-bike extends the range when cycling. As with knowledge, the value of technologies is heavily dependent on how well they fit their purpose and how up-to-date they are. Advances in battery technology, for example, have a significant impact on the value of e-bikes.

What Are Important (Future) Technologies?

Future technologies like the next versions of artificial intelligence will probably change the way you work and how you design products fundamentally. However, the newest technology is not always the best. For example: A small grocery store has two checkouts, and aisles lead to each of them. If more than 3 customers are queuing at the first checkout, they ring a small bell hanging there. Immediately, the second checkout is staffed. This little bell is perfect for that purpose, any digital solution would be pointless.

Technologies must support the needs and expectations of all affected interest groups. More and more organizations implement new digital solutions to improve their own efficiency and neglect their customers. For example: An insurance company introduces a digital portal. Customers must use this portal for any communication, say, to download letters from the insurance company or to upload invoices. This solution significantly increases the efficiency of customer processes for the insurance company, but it charges their customers for the corresponding activities. Most customers do not even notice this disadvantage because the insurance company cleverly advertises this "modern digital solution" as a customer benefit.

Technologies must support the processes as ideally as possible. If processes are changed through a higher degree of automation, the technologies must be adapted. For example: During the COVID-19 pandemic, many learning processes were switched to remote teaching before the required technologies such as modern-end devices or high-performance internet were available. In addition, many people had to learn how to use the technologies effectively before the learning process. So, when changing technology, you have a lot to consider to ensure it's truly more valuable than the existing technology.

"The best technology is the one you don't notice."

—Pablo Picasso, Painter

Here are some future technologies that may have significant impact on our lives and society:

- Artificial intelligence can support humans in many ways—it can be used to automate repetitive tasks, enhance decision-making, boost creativity, strengthen education, or assist in daily life.

- Blockchain technology is a distributed database that securely and transparently records transactions between users and makes them resistant to manipulation (or at least tries to).

- Non-fungible tokens (NFTs) are digital certificates of authenticity for unique virtual objects or artworks that record their ownership and originality in the blockchain, similar to an artist signing their original painting.

- Internet of Things (IoT) enables organizations to connect and monitor devices, gather real-time data, automate processes, and optimize operations, leading to improved efficiency, cost savings, and informed decision-making.

- Robotics helps organizations automate repetitive tasks, enhance precision, improve productivity, and reduce operational costs while enabling innovations in manufacturing, healthcare, logistics, and more.

- Quantum computing uses quantum mechanics to perform calculations that are not possible with conventional computers. This can have significant implications for the development of materials, drugs, and artificial intelligence.

- Renewable energy sources such as solar, wind, and green hydrogen produced from renewable energy sources have a huge potential to replace fossil fuels as the primary energy source on our planet in near future.

- Biotechnology enables organizations to harness biological processes and technologies to innovate in healthcare, agriculture, and environmental sustainability, driving advancements in medicine or food production.

- With advancements in 3D printing, you may soon be able to create functional organs, revolutionizing healthcare by saving lives, much like how this technology is already transforming production or the creation of custom jewelry.

- Augmented Reality (AR) and Virtual Reality (VR): These advancements will transform the ways you learn, work, and experience the world. AR and VR offer immersive solutions that can enhance education, healthcare, and entertainment.

The value of technologies always depends on the extent to which they fit the problem and task. Here is an example of an expensive and unsustainable technology that is used by hundreds of millions of people around the world every day, even though it has many disadvantages: traditional air-cooling for hot countries.

Radiation cooling is a relatively simple, alternative technology. It offers a sustainable, cost-effective, and health-conscious alternative to traditional air-cooling (and air-conditioning). It provides a comfortable and uniform temperature and a healthier environment, and it operates silently. It consumes significantly less electricity, requires less maintenance, and offers long-term savings. And since it does not use any (harmful) refrigerants, it is eco-friendly and minimizes water usage due to its closed-loop cooling system. Radiation cooling can even be retrofitted in existing buildings.

Despite all of these obvious advantages, radiation cooling is not widely used. The demand for simple and energy-efficient air-cooling systems will increase significantly in the future due to global warming.

What Are Other Resources and Why Do You Need Them?

In addition to the resources mentioned so far, there are other resources that many organizations use and need in order to be successful. Here are some of them:

Financial Resources:

- Capital for investments in infrastructure, technology, and operations.
- Access to credit, funding, and financial reserves for risk management.
- Budget allocation and cost management plans.

Physical Resources:

- Tangible assets like facilities, equipment, machinery and raw materials.
- Infrastructure to support production, distribution or service delivery.
- Environmental resources like water, air, solar and wind energy, plants, animals, minerals and metals.

Intellectual Resources:

- Proprietary knowledge, patents, trademarks, and intellectual property.
- Organizational know-how, good practices and innovative processes.
- Brand reputation and customer loyalty as intangible assets.

Handle Important Operational Risks with Care

The need to evaluate risks at a high level was discussed in STEP 3, as a critical input before the final plan can be released and implemented. Since risks also occur on operational levels, responsible organizations need to manage those risks (at low level) in the same professional way as planning risks (at high level). Examples of process-related, operational risks are:

Human-Related Risks

- Errors and mistakes: Incorrect data entry, miscommunication or failure to follow procedures.
- Lack of coordination: Poor collaboration between departments or interest groups caused by information silos, impeding process efficiency.

- Skill gaps: Employees lacking the necessary training or expertise to perform tasks effectively.
- Non-adherence: Failure to comply with established processes or Standard Operating Procedures (SOPs).

Technology Risks

- Operational system failures: Downtime or malfunction of IT systems critical to operations.
- Integration issues: Problems with compatibility between systems or tools used in processes.
- Outdated technology: Inefficiencies due to reliance on obsolete software or hardware.

Supply Chain Risks

- Supplier delays: Late delivery of materials or services impacting production schedules.
- Quality Issues: Defective or substandard inputs leading to rework, product failures and cost.
- Transportation disruptions: Operational logistics challenges such as delays, accidents, or loss of goods.

Compliance and Regulatory Risks

- Non-Compliance: Failure to adhere to industry standards, laws or regulations.
- Audit Findings: Process weaknesses identified during inspections or audits.
- Documentation Gaps: Missing or incomplete records required for compliance.

Process Design Risks

- Inefficient processes: Overly complex or redundant workflows or interface problems, wasting time and resources.
- Bottlenecks: Points in the process where work slows down due to capacity constraints.
- Lack of Scalability: Processes unable to handle increased demand without significant disruptions.

Operational Quality Risks

- Product defects: Operational errors leading to non-conformance with quality standards.
- Inspection failures: Insufficient quality control measures that overlook critical deficiencies.
- Rework and waste: Time and resources spent fixing errors, increasing costs.

Resource Management Risks

- Resource shortages: Inadequate availability of key materials, services or equipment.
- Capacity overload: Overburdening processes, leading to delays and reduced quality.
- Improper resource allocation: Mismanagement of resources, causing inefficiencies.

Data and Information Risks

- Inaccurate Data: Use of outdated or incorrect information leading to faulty decision-making.
- Loss of data: Missing critical records due to system failures or human error.

- Unauthorized access: Data breaches compromising operational integrity.

To manage operational risks, the same risk management principles apply as for high-level success-related risks (STEP 3).

Step 1: Risk Identification

Select those operational risks that are relevant for your organization.

Step 2: Risk Assessment

Classify selected risks, e.g., according to probability and impact.

Step 3: Preventive Measures

Check measures that can avoid or mitigate risks, and improve them.

Step 4: Crisis and Emergency Management

Prepare and test crisis and emergency management.

Step 5: Continuity Management

Prepare restoration of normal operation.

"Only a fool learns from his own mistakes. The wise man learns from the mistakes of others."

—Otto von Bismarck, First Chancellor of the German Empire

Always Act Sustainably

Sustainability includes reconciling environmental protection, social fairness and economic stability, often referred to as the three pillars of sustainability: Environmental (E), Social (S), and Governance (G). This balance ensures that current needs are met without compromising the ability of future generations to meet their own needs.

The 17 Sustainable Development Goals (SDGs), adopted by the United Nations in 2015, act as the "mother framework" of ESG by providing a comprehensive global roadmap designed to address key challenges like poverty, inequality, climate change, environmental degradation, and peace by 2030. They are part of the 2030 Agenda for Sustainable Development, which all 193 UN member states agreed upon.

Each of the three ESG pillars of sustainability relate to a selection of the 17 SDGs. Together, all three pillars fully support the SDG framework. Here are some advantages of using the ESG pillars over the original SDGs in certain contexts:

The ESG pillars are simpler and more focused for businesses. This simplicity makes ESG easier for organizations to adopt, measure and report, especially for corporate decision-makers and investors.

The ESG pillars are tailored for financial markets. Investors use ESG metrics to evaluate sustainability performance, risk mitigation, and value creation, making it a practical tool for businesses to attract sustainable investments.

The ESG framework can be adapted to specific sectors and organizational needs, unlike the SDGs, which are broad and universal.

ESG metrics are specific and quantifiable, making it easier for organizations to track progress and demonstrate results.

ESG frameworks are often tied to standards like GRI, SASB, or TCFD, which provide detailed guidelines for reporting.

"We do not inherit the earth from our ancestors, but borrow it from our children."

—Antoine de Saint-Exupéry, Writer and Pilot

Ensure Sustainable Environmental Responsibility (E)

The Environmental (E) pillar focuses on the planet and its resources. The related SDGs aim to address environmental challenges like resource depletion, climate change, biodiversity loss and unsustainable infrastructure. The following SDGs reflect the environmental focus in ESG, driving efforts toward sustainability, conservation, and addressing global ecological challenges:

Resource management

SDG 6: Clean water and sanitation

SDG 7: Affordable and clean energy

SDG 12: Responsible consumption and production

Climate responsibility

SDG 13: Climate action

Biodiversity protection

SDG 14: Life below water

SDG 15: Life on land

Sustainable cities and communities

SDG 11: Sustainable buildings and affordable housing

What You Can Do in Practice to Act Responsibly

SDG 6: Ensure availability and sustainable management of water and sanitation.

What you can do:

- Install water-saving technologies and recycle wastewater in facilities.
- Invest in clean water infrastructure, filtration systems or sanitation facilities.
- Partner with NGOs and other organizations to scale water conservation projects.
- Run campaigns to educate employees, communities and customers about water conservation practices.

SDG 7: Ensure access to affordable, reliable, sustainable, and modern energy.

What you can do:

- Transition to solar, wind, and derived clean energy sources like green hydrogen to power vehicles and facilities.
- Retrofit buildings with energy-efficient technologies like sustainable air-conditioning systems, LED lighting and energy management software.
- Commit to measurable targets, such as becoming carbon neutral or producing all energy from renewable sources by a specific year.

SDG 12: Ensure responsible consumption and production.

What you can do:

- Adopt circular economy practices by designing products for durability, repairability, and recyclability or implementing recycling programs.
- Implement zero-waste policies in operations by minimizing packaging, reducing food waste, or reusing manufacturing by-products.
- Promote sustainable consumption by providing eco-labeling, transparency about product lifecycles, and awareness campaigns.

SDG 13: Take urgent action to combat climate change and its impacts.

What you can do:

- Commit to reducing greenhouse gas emissions by transitioning to renewable energy, improve energy efficiency, and set carbon neutrality goals.
- Develop and offer climate-friendly products or services; e.g., energy-efficient appliances, sustainable transportation, and air-cooling solutions.

- Develop plans to minimize climate risks (e.g., supply chain disruptions due to extreme weather) by sourcing locally or investing in climate-resilient infrastructure.

SDG 14: Conserve and sustainably use oceans, seas and marine resources.

What you can do:

- Eliminate single-use plastics in operations and packaging, replacing them with sustainable alternatives.
- Support the preservation of marine ecosystems by avoiding overfished species.
- Invest in projects that protect coral reefs, mangroves, and other critical marine habitats.

SDG 15: Protect, restore, and promote sustainable use of terrestrial ecosystems, forests, and biodiversity.

What you can do:

- Implement sustainable sourcing of raw materials like timber, palm oil or paper to avoid deforestation and land degradation.
- Participate in or fund tree-planting initiatives and habitat restoration projects to offset environmental impacts and enhance biodiversity.
- Protect endangered species and habitats by funding wildlife conservation programs. Avoid using harmful chemicals that threaten biodiversity.

SDG 11: Sustainable urban infrastructure and safe, affordable housing

What you can do:

- Invest in sustainable building designs using eco-friendly technologies and sustainable air-conditioning systems. Support urban green projects.

- Support sustainable vehicles (e.g., with EV, FCEV or HICE technology) and related infrastructure (charging or hydrogen-filling stations) to encourage sustainable transport.
- Collaborate with non-profits to build affordable housing that integrates sustainable energy solutions and access to essential services.

Ensure Sustainable Social Responsibility (S)

The Social (S) pillar of ESG focuses on people, communities, and societal well-being, aligning with several Sustainable Development Goals (SDGs) that address human rights, equity, and inclusivity. Here's how the SDGs map to the "Social" category in ESG, emphasizing the importance of creating positive societal impacts while addressing inequality, health, and education.

Human rights and equality

SDG 1: No poverty

SDG 5: Gender equality

SDG 10: Reduced inequalities

Health and safety

SDG 3: Good health and well-being

Education and skill development

SDG 4: Quality education

Decent work and economic inclusion

SDG 8: Decent work and economic growth

Food security and poverty reduction

SDG 2: Zero hunger

What You Can Do in Practice to Act Responsibly

SDG 1: Eradicate extreme poverty and ensure economic security for all.

What you can do:

- Ensure all employees, including those in supply chains, receive fair wages and benefits that support a decent standard of living.
- Partner with local governments and NGOs to build infrastructure, such as schools, housing and healthcare facilities, in impoverished areas.
- Donate or subsidize products and services (e.g., food, water, shelter) for underprivileged communities. Support affordable microfinance initiatives.

SDG 5: Achieve gender equality and empower all women and girls.

What you can do:

- Ensure equal pay for equal work, eliminate gender pay gaps and provide opportunities for women to advance into leadership roles.
- Establish zero-tolerance policies for harassment and discrimination, backed by clear reporting mechanisms. Offer flexible arrangements for shift workers.
- Ensure fair labor practices and equal opportunities for women, also in supply chains. Offer childcare support to help balance work and family responsibilities.

SDG 10: Reduce inequalities within and among countries.

What you can do:

- Create diversity and inclusion programs to hire and support people from underrepresented groups, including minorities and individuals with disabilities.

- Ensure fair wages and career advancement opportunities regardless of gender, race, ethnicity or socioeconomic background.

- Develop or support affordable and accessible products or services for underserved populations, such as low-income families or remote communities.

SDG 3: Ensure healthy lives and promote well-being for all at all ages.

What you can do:

- Offer comprehensive health insurance, mental health resources and healthy meals. Create a supportive work environment that prioritizes work-life balance.

- Partner with NGOs and governments to fund or provide affordable healthcare services, especially in underserved regions.

- Develop technologies, products or services that improve healthcare delivery or reduce costs, such as telemedicine platforms or affordable medications.

SDG 4: Provide inclusive, equitable and quality education for lifelong learning.

What you can do:

- Offer continuous learning opportunities, such as professional certifications, technical skill training or leadership development.

- Supply learning materials for children in low-income regions. Partner with NGOs to create education programs for marginalized populations.

- Provide affordable technology solutions (e.g., tablets, internet access) to bridge the digital divide and enhance e-learning opportunities.

SDG 8: Promote sustained economic growth and decent work for all.

What you can do:

- Guarantee fair pay, safe working environments, and adherence to labor laws.
- Conduct regular audits to ensure compliance with ethical labor practices.
- Invest in local communities by creating job opportunities. Provide training programs to upskill workers and enhance employability.
- Develop programs that support small businesses and startups. Provide access to funding, mentoring and tools to help entrepreneurs succeed.

SDG 2: End hunger, achieve food security, and promote sustainable agriculture.

What you can do:

- Support technologies to optimize food production, storage and distribution, ensuring that less food is wasted.
- Partner with farmers to implement sustainable farming techniques like crop rotation, water conservation, and organic farming.
- Develop affordable and nutritious food products for underserved populations, especially in low-income regions and combat malnutrition.

Ensure Sustainable Governance (G)

The **Governance (G)** pillar of ESG focuses on ethical leadership, corporate accountability, transparency, and adherence to laws and regulations. It aligns with several **Sustainable Development Goals (SDGs)** that address governance, justice, and partnerships. Here's how the SDGs map to the "Governance" category in ESG, highlighting the importance of ethical and transparent operations, fostering trust, and accountability in organizations.

Corporate transparency and accountability

SDG 16: Peace, justice and strong institutions

Innovation and sustainable practices

SDG 9: Industry, innovation and infrastructure

Collaborate leadership

SDG 17: Partnerships for the goals

What You Can Do in Practice to Act Responsibly

SDG 16: Promote peaceful and inclusive societies, access to justice and effective governance.

What you can do:

- Establish and enforce strong ethical policies to prevent bribery, corruption and fraud. Ensure transparency in reporting and decision-making processes.
- Partner with NGOs or governments to fund legal aid programs for vulnerable populations, ensuring access to justice for all.
- Support initiatives that foster social cohesion, reduce violence and promote conflict resolution. Fund educational programs to teach young people the importance of peace and justice.

SDG 9: Build resilient infrastructure, promote sustainable industrialization, and foster innovation.

What you can do:

- Develop eco-friendly infrastructure, renewable energy facilities, and sustainable transportation systems.

- Use innovative materials and technologies to make infrastructure projects more sustainable and resilient to climate change.

- Support small and medium enterprises (SMEs) by providing access to funding, technology, and training to drive sustainable economic growth.

SDG 17: Strengthen global partnerships to achieve the goals.

What you can do:

- Partner with non-profits and international organizations to co-develop solutions for sustainable development challenges, such as poverty, health, and climate change.

- Join multi-interest group partnerships to address global challenges collectively, such as through shared sustainability goals, pooled resources, and knowledge-sharing.

- Share expertise, innovations, and technologies with developing countries to help them build capacity and achieve sustainable development goals.

How to Measure the Success of Your Sustainability Initiatives

If you use the right indicators, you can quickly determine in which areas you have made progress toward success and where there is still room for improvement. This allows you to optimize your sustainability plan in a targeted manner. It can make sense to define sustainability initiatives as process improvement projects. One example could be a project to significantly improve the sustainability by decarbonizing the supply chain processes. The success goal could be to reduce the CO_2 footprint of your tier-1 supply chain by 20% within 6 months, to support SDG #13 (climate action).

Progress toward this goal would be measured with performance indicators at project milestones. Examples of indicators could be the reduction in

CO_2 emissions per supplier, the percentage of suppliers engaged in the decarbonizing project, the percentage of suppliers who have switched to renewable energy sources, or the total investment of suppliers in decarbonizing technology.

At the end of your sustainability project, your tier-1 supply chain processes would be more sustainable. This success could be cleverly used for marketing. The next sustainability project could be to further improve the decarbonization of the tier-1 supply chain, and to include some tier-2 suppliers in your project.

A Strong Plan Is Only as Good as Its Execution

KAIZUNO ensures that businesses don't get stuck in "plan mode" but instead take practical action—building strong teams, securing partnerships, and using data-driven decision-making.

As Maya Dani put her vision into action, she faced real-world challenges—unexpected costs, supplier issues, and team struggles. Let's return to her story and see how she tackled them.

Pursue Practical Implementation (STEP 4) - Application

Be a Competent Team that Enjoys Working Together

When I first started Mirabelle, I believed that hiring skilled employees was the key to success, but I quickly realized something important. A team that works well together is more valuable than a group of individually talented people. I had team members with impressive résumés, but some didn't collaborate well, while others lacked motivation.

That's when I learned: Competence alone isn't enough. Success comes from a team that is skilled, aligned, and enjoys working together.

The Moment I Knew Team Culture Mattered

One evening, two of my best employees—Luis (head chef) and Sofia (front desk manager)—had a heated argument over a last-minute VIP request. Sofia had promised a customized private dinner, but Luis, overwhelmed with a busy service, wasn't informed early enough. The result was a frustrated chef, a flustered front desk team, and VIP guest experience that felt chaotic instead of seamless. I realized that lack of teamwork, not lack of talent, was hurting our guest experience.

That day, I made a commitment: Mirabelle wouldn't just have skilled employees; it would have a strong, collaborative team.

The Three Elements of a Strong Team

To transform our team culture, I focused on three things:

1. Competence: Hire the Right Skills and Train Continuously

Does everyone have the necessary expertise for their role?

Do we provide continuous learning opportunities?

Are we placing people in positions where they thrive?

How we applied this at Mirabelle:

- We implemented cross-training, so employees understood different roles (e.g., front desk learned basic restaurant service, and vice versa).
- We encouraged team members to attend hospitality workshops and courses.
- We hired not just for skills, but for attitude, adaptability, and willingness to learn.

2. Collaboration: Build a Culture of Communication and Support

Does every team member understand how their role impacts others?

Do departments communicate effectively?

Are we solving problems together rather than blaming each other?

How we applied this at Mirabelle:

- We introduced daily "5-minute team syncs" to align operations across departments.
- We created "open feedback loops" where employees could suggest improvements without fear.
- We launched team bonding activities to build trust and relationships outside of work.

3. Enjoyment: Make Work Fulfilling and Fun

Do employees feel valued and motivated?

Is the work environment positive and encouraging?

Do we celebrate wins and progress together?

How we applied this at Mirabelle:

- We introduced "Employee Appreciation Days" to recognize outstanding work.
- We encouraged autonomy and creativity—allowing employees to bring their own ideas to enhance guest experience.
- We fostered a culture where everyone felt like they belonged—a team, not just coworkers.

The Impact: How Team Transformation Changed Everything

With these changes, service improved because communication was smoother, employee morale skyrocketed because they felt part of something meaningful, and guest satisfaction increased because happy employees created a better experience.

One guest, after experiencing how seamless and welcoming our team was, told me: "It feels like everyone at Mirabelle actually enjoys working here—like they genuinely care about the experience."

That's when I knew—we had created something special.

Final Lesson: A Strong Team Is a Happy, Aligned, and Skilled Team

- Competence is necessary—but teamwork is what makes a business thrive.
- Collaboration eliminates friction and creates a seamless experience.
- When employees enjoy their work, guests feel it too.

At Mirabelle, we don't just hire employees, we build a team that grows, collaborates, and succeeds together.

Secure Support of Strong Partners and Suppliers

At Mirabelle, I quickly learned that a hotel's success isn't just about great service and a welcoming atmosphere—it's also about having the right partners and suppliers who share your vision. No business operates in isolation. The quality, reliability, and ethics of our suppliers and business partners directly impacted our ability to deliver exceptional guest experiences.

That's when I realized: Success isn't just about choosing partners—it's about securing the right ones and building long-term, mutually beneficial relationships.

The Wake-Up Call: When a Supplier Let Us Down

Early on, I made the mistake of choosing the cheapest supplier for our in-room coffee and breakfast pastries. Everything seemed fine—until one weekend, during peak season, our supplier failed to deliver. Guests expecting a fresh morning experience got instant coffee and store-bought croissants. The team scrambled to find last-minute replacements, but our reputation suffered, and I had to personally apologize to guests.

That's when I learned: Strong suppliers aren't just about price—they're about reliability, quality, and shared values. From that moment, I committed to securing only the best partners—ones who wouldn't just provide products but who would be invested in our success.

How to Secure the Right Partners and Suppliers

I developed a three-step framework for choosing and securing strong partnerships:

Step 1: Define What Makes a Good Partner

What do we need beyond just products?

Does this supplier align with our quality, ethics, and sustainability values?

Can they scale and adapt as our business grows?

Example: Instead of choosing the cheapest bakery supplier, we partnered with a local artisan baker who could guarantee fresh, high-quality pastries every morning. We chose reliability over cost-cutting, consistency in service, and a partner who shared our passion for quality.

Step 2: Build Strong, Mutually Beneficial Relationships

How can we ensure long-term loyalty with our suppliers?

Are we treating them as partners, not just vendors?

How can we make our business valuable to them, too?

How we applied this at Mirabelle:

- We committed to long-term contracts with suppliers who provided consistent quality.
- We collaborated on seasonal products—such as featuring our bakery's exclusive *Mirabelle Signature Pastries.*
- We promoted our suppliers in our marketing (e.g., mentioning them in our guest welcome booklets).

The result was that suppliers prioritized us over other clients. They worked with us to innovate new offerings, and we became part of their success story, not just another customer.

Step 3: Always Have Backup Plans and Alternative Suppliers

What happens if a supplier fails?

Do we have emergency alternatives?

How can we protect ourselves from disruptions?

For example, after our first supplier failure, we established backup partnerships with two additional bakeries; created a supplier contingency plan for key items like coffee, linens, and fresh produce; and maintained an emergency supply stock for critical items. The next time a supplier delay happened, we were ready. Instead of a crisis, it was a seamless switch to our backup supplier—guests never even noticed.

The Impact: Why Strong Partnerships Changed Everything

Once we secured reliable, high-quality partners, we saw a huge transformation in how Mirabelle operated. Guest satisfaction increased because product quality was consistently excellent, operational stress decreased because we weren't constantly firefighting supplier issues, and suppliers prioritized us because we treated them as valued partners.

One of our suppliers, a local organic farm, told me: "Maya, we love working with Mirabelle because you don't just buy from us—you support our growth too. That's why we always give you the best of what we have."

That's when I knew—securing the right partners wasn't just about business; it was about building a network of trust, reliability, and shared success.

Final Lesson: Strong Partners Make a Business Stronger

- Cheap suppliers cost more in the long run.
- Reliable, aligned partners create lasting success.
- Loyalty works both ways—treat your partners well, and they will invest in your growth.
- Always have a backup plan—because even the best suppliers can face challenges.

At Mirabelle, we don't just find suppliers, we secure strong partners who help us grow, innovate, and succeed—together.

Maintain a Supportive Leadership

When I first opened Mirabelle, I thought being a leader meant making decisions, solving problems, and giving instructions, but over time, I realized something important: A great leader doesn't just lead—they support, empower, and uplift their team.

A business isn't successful because of the owner alone. It thrives when the people within it feel valued, motivated, and inspired to do their best work. That's when I shifted from being a boss to being a supportive leader.

The Turning Point: When I Almost Lost My Best Employee

One of my most dedicated employees, Sofia, had been with Mirabelle since the beginning. She was the kind of manager every business owner dreams of—efficient, reliable, and deeply committed to our vision.

One afternoon, she knocked on my office door. "Maya, I need to talk to you."

I could tell she was nervous.

"I've been feeling exhausted. I love working here, but I'm struggling. Sometimes, I feel like no one notices how much effort I put in. I don't know if I can keep doing this."

Her words hit me hard. She wasn't asking for a higher salary or fewer hours. She was asking for recognition, support, and leadership that made her feel valued.

That day, I realized: Being a leader isn't just about running a business; it's about taking care of the people who make it work.

What Makes a Good Leader?

I changed the way I led Mirabelle by focusing on five key leadership principles that I had overlooked before:

1. Adaptability in the Face of Uncertainty

A great leader doesn't just follow a fixed plan—they adapt when challenges arise. Leadership isn't about avoiding uncertainty; it's about using it as an opportunity to innovate.

How I applied this at Mirabelle:

- When COVID-19 disrupted our business, I quickly pivoted our model—transforming rooms into remote workspaces and launching staycation packages.
- I embraced agility, ensuring that my team knew we could navigate change together.

The result? We didn't just survive the crisis—we found new revenue streams and guest segments that we continue serving today.

2. Intuitive Foresight

A strong leader doesn't just react—they anticipate future trends and shifts.

How I applied this at Mirabelle:

- I kept a close eye on hospitality trends, learning from leading hotels and industry experts.
- We introduced mobile check-in and AI-powered guest insights before they became industry standards.

The result? We stayed ahead of guest expectations instead of playing catch-up.

3. Empathetic Conflict Resolution

Great leaders recognize and resolve conflicts early before they escalate. Understanding both sides of an issue builds trust and long-term loyalty.

How I applied this at Mirabelle:

- When a dispute arose between the front desk and kitchen teams over last-minute guest requests, I didn't take sides—I listened to both perspectives.
- We introduced a cross-departmental communication system to prevent future misalignment.

The result was stronger collaboration and fewer internal tensions—which meant smoother service for our guests.

4. Silent Resilience

Leadership isn't about loud speeches—it's about calm, steady confidence during tough times. When leaders stay composed, their team feels safe and motivated.

How I applied this at Mirabelle:

- During our first overbooking crisis, my instinct was to panic. Instead, I focused on solutions, not stress.
- I calmly reassured my team, quickly arranged alternate accommodations for guests, and handled the situation professionally.

The result? Instead of a PR disaster, we won guest loyalty through proactive service recovery.

5. Encouraging Initiative

Instead of micromanaging, great leaders empower their teams to take ownership. Mistakes aren't failures—they're learning opportunities.

How I applied this at Mirabelle:

- We allowed employees to make guest experience decisions without waiting for approval on small things.
- We encouraged team-led innovation—if an employee had an idea to improve the hotel, we tested it.
- We provided leadership training, so team members could grow into bigger roles.

The result was employees felt ownership and responsibility for their work, leading to higher engagement and better performance.

The Impact: How Supportive Leadership Transformed Mirabelle

Employee turnover decreased because people felt valued and heard, service improved because employees were empowered to make guests happy, and the work environment became positive and collaborative.

One day, a guest told me: "I've never seen a hotel where employees actually seem happy to be here. It makes a difference in the experience." That's when

I knew—leadership isn't about control. It's about creating an environment where people can thrive.

Final Lesson: A Leader's Job Is to Lift Others Up

Employees don't leave bad jobs. They leave bad leadership. Supportive leadership creates loyalty, engagement, and a thriving workplace. When leaders empower their team, the whole business flourishes.

At Mirabelle, we don't just manage employees, we support, recognize, and empower them—because when our team succeeds, the entire business succeeds.

Treat Each Other Well

At Mirabelle, I quickly learned that how employees treat each other behind the scenes affects the entire guest experience. A hotel can have the best rooms, the best design, and the best service policies—but if the team doesn't respect and support each other, everything falls apart. That's when I realized a thriving business isn't just built on excellent service—it's built on a culture of kindness, respect, and teamwork.

The Moment I Knew Team Culture Mattered

One afternoon, I overheard a tense conversation between two employees—Daniel, a housekeeper, and Lisa, a front desk receptionist. Lisa had just received a complaint from a guest about a missing towel in their room, and she turned to Daniel, frustrated.

Lisa: "You need to be more careful, Daniel. We can't keep having these issues!"

Daniel: "Maybe if you actually gave us the right room assignments on time, this wouldn't happen!"

A guest standing nearby overheard everything. That day, I knew it wasn't enough to focus on guest treatment; we needed to focus on how we treated each other as well. If employees didn't communicate with respect and kindness, guests feel the tension.

That's when I made a decision: "Treat Each Other Well" would become a core value at Mirabelle.

What Is a Supportive Corporate Culture and Why Does It Matter?

A company's culture is like a family dynamic—the way people interact, communicate, and work together defines the overall experience. A positive workplace culture does more than just improve employee satisfaction, it drives productivity, retention, and innovation.

Organizations with strong cultures attract and retain top talent, reduce workplace conflicts, and increase overall motivation and job satisfaction. Boosting customer experience through happier employees is a great strategy.

Company culture isn't a "soft" business factor, it's a key driver of long-term success. I realized that to truly embed this at Mirabelle, we had to take intentional steps to build a supportive culture.

How We Built a Culture of Respect and Kindness

To make "treating each other well" a daily habit at Mirabelle, we focused on three key principles:

1. Encourage Open and Respectful Communication

- Do employees feel comfortable speaking up without fear of judgment?
- Do team members communicate clearly and kindly, even under pressure?

- Is there a culture of active listening?

How we applied this at Mirabelle:

We introduced a "clear and kind communication" rule—every employee was trained to give feedback respectfully. We implemented conflict resolution workshops, teaching employees how to handle disagreements professionally. We encouraged "pause before reacting"—helping employees respond thoughtfully rather than emotionally.

The result was that employees started solving problems together instead of blaming each other.

2. Foster a Culture of Appreciation

- Do employees feel recognized for their contributions?
- Are small acts of kindness encouraged?
- Does leadership lead by example in showing appreciation?

How we applied this at Mirabelle:

We created a "shout-out board" where employees could publicly appreciate each other.

We introduced a monthly "Kindness Champion" award, recognizing those who went out of their way to support their colleagues. I made it a personal habit to thank employees daily—whether for handling a guest complaint well or simply for their hard work.

The result was that employees started valuing each other more.

One day, Lisa (the receptionist from the earlier argument) wrote on the shout-out board: "Big thanks to Daniel for always going the extra mile. I see how hard you work, and I appreciate it!" That's when I knew we were building something special.

3. Create a Safe and Inclusive Work Environment

- Does everyone feel like they belong?
- Are all voices heard and respected?
- Are there zero-tolerance policies for toxic behavior?

How we applied this at Mirabelle:

We trained managers to identify and stop toxic workplace behaviors before they escalated. We made sure every employee had a voice—from housekeepers to senior managers. We reinforced zero tolerance for discrimination, gossip, or workplace bullying.

The result was that when people felt safe and included, they contributed their best.

What Makes a Great Workplace Culture?

A supportive culture is built on key behaviors that define how an organization operates daily.

A strong workplace culture:

- Has a resilient foundation of values, with leaders as role models.
- Promotes open feedback, mutual appreciation, and mindfulness.
- Supports transparent communication to strengthen trust and cooperation.
- Increases motivation and commitment by rewarding and celebrating success.
- Values diversity and inclusion, appreciating different perspectives and ideas.
- Encourages sustainability and innovation.
- Supports flexible working models to improve work-life balance.
- Enables collaboration across teams and departments.

Culture is a conscious and continuous investment by leadership, not just a one-time initiative.

The Impact: How Treating Each Other Well Transformed Mirabelle

Teamwork improved. Departments worked together instead of against each other. Guest satisfaction increased because a happy team delivers better service. The workplace became a place people actually wanted to be.

One of our employees, Maria, told me: "Maya, I've worked in other hotels before, but this is the first time I've actually felt respected and valued at work." That's when I knew: Culture isn't just about leadership; it's about how people treat each other every single day.

Final Lesson: A Thriving Workplace Starts with Kindness

Respect and kindness between employees leads to better guest experiences. A toxic work environment hurts the business more than any external competition. When people feel valued, they work harder, stay longer, and support each other more.

At Mirabelle, we didn't just build a business. We built a team that treats each other with kindness, respect, and appreciation because that's what true success looks like.

Ensure Good Process Management

When I first started Hotel Mirabelle, I thought success came from passion, great service, and a strong team. While those things mattered, I soon learned a crucial truth that even the best team will struggle if processes are unclear, inefficient, or chaotic.

Great guest experiences don't happen by accident. They happen when every part of the business runs smoothly and when employees know exactly what to do, when to do it, and how to do it.

That's when I realized a well-run business isn't about working harder; it's about working smarter with strong processes in place.

The Moment I Realized We Needed Better Processes

One morning, we had a VIP guest checking in at 10 AM. Everything seemed fine, until the room wasn't ready because housekeeping didn't get an early check-in alert and the welcome amenities were missing because the front desk forgot to notify the kitchen. The guest arrived, frustrated, and I had to step in to apologize.

It wasn't that my team was unskilled. Our processes were broken. That day, I knew we didn't just need better people; we needed better process management.

What Good Process Management Looks Like

I focused on three key areas to make Hotel Mirabelle run like a well-oiled machine:

1. Standardize Repetitive Tasks

- Do employees know exactly what needs to happen for routine tasks?
- Is there a checklist for key processes?
- Are roles and responsibilities clear?

How we applied this at Mirabelle:

We created step-by-step Standard Operating Procedures (SOPs) for housekeeping, check-ins, guest complaints, and breakfast service. We implemented daily checklists for each department to track responsibilities, and we introduced pre-shift briefings, so every employee knew the priorities for the day.

The result was that everyone was on the same page, and mistakes became rare.

2. Separate Value-Adding vs. Supporting Processes

- Which processes directly impact guests?
- Which processes support the main experience?
- Are supporting processes optimized to enhance the value chain?

How we applied this at Mirabelle:

We highlighted value-adding processes (direct guest impact)

Reservations and check-ins → Guests expect a seamless arrival.

Housekeeping and room preparation → Clean rooms create the first impression.

Food and beverage service → Guests care about meal quality, variety, and service speed.

We added supporting processes (backend operations)

Inventory and supplier management → Ensures smooth kitchen and room service.

Employee training →Employee performance depends on proper onboarding and coaching.

Technology and IT maintenance → Ensures booking systems and digital check-ins work.

Understanding the difference between value-adding and supporting processes helped us allocate time, budget, and improvements effectively.

3. Automate and Streamline Where Possible

- Are we wasting time on manual tasks that technology can handle?
- Can we automate processes to reduce errors?
- How do we make things more efficient?

How we applied this at Mirabelle:

We integrated a real-time communication system so the front desk, housekeeping, and kitchen teams were instantly updated on guest needs. We switched to automated booking confirmations and payment processing, eliminating human error. We introduced a digital maintenance request system, ensuring reported issues were tracked and resolved faster.

The result was that employees spent less time on paperwork and more time with guests.

4. Measure and Improve Performance Continuously

- How do we track if processes are working?
- Are we using real performance indicators to measure success?
- How do we make ongoing improvements?

How we applied this at Mirabelle:

We set up Key Performance Indicators (KPIs) for check-in times, housekeeping response times, and guest satisfaction scores. We introduced a benchmarking process, comparing our service times with competitor hotels and identifying areas for improvement. We started monthly KPI review meetings, where we analyzed trends and adapted strategies based on performance data.

Example: When we noticed that our average check-in time was 20% longer than competitor hotels, we introduced pre-arrival online check-ins, reducing check-in times from 7 minutes to 4 minutes.

Example: We monitored guest feedback and realized that breakfast service felt slow. We restructured kitchen workflows and reduced serving time by 30%, improving overall guest satisfaction scores.

5. Implement Continuous Process Improvements (Kaizen and PDCA)

- Do we have a system for regularly improving processes?
- Are employees involved in suggesting and implementing process improvements?
- Do we test improvements before fully rolling them out?

How we applied this at Mirabelle:

We trained employees in Kaizen and the PDCA cycle (Plan-Do-Check-Act) to empower them to suggest and implement small improvements. We introduced "5 Whys" problem-solving to find the root cause of inefficiencies. We tested small process changes first, ensuring no disruption before scaling improvements.

The result was that Mirabelle began to run on a culture of continuous improvement.

The Impact: How Process Management Transformed Mirabelle

With process management, there were fewer mistakes, faster service, and smoother operations. Employees felt less stressed because expectations were clear. Guest satisfaction improved because service felt effortless.

One returning guest told me: "I've stayed at Mirabelle before, but this time, everything felt even more polished and smooth. It's like the hotel runs perfectly now." That's when I knew that great process management doesn't just improve efficiency, it creates a better experience for everyone.

Final Lesson: Processes Build Excellence

A well-structured business prevents stress, mistakes, and delays. Clear processes empower employees to focus on what matters—delivering great service. The best hotels don't just provide luxury. They provide seamless, predictable, and high-quality experiences through strong processes.

At Hotel Mirabelle, we don't just work hard; we work smart because great process management turns chaos into excellence.

Provide Attractive Products and Services

When I first opened Mirabelle, I believed that great customer service would set us apart. I thought warm hospitality and friendly employees would be enough to make guests return. But I quickly learned service alone isn't enough. You need products and services that people truly want. Even if guests loved our hospitality, they wouldn't return unless we gave them an experience worth coming back for. That's when I realized that people don't just book a hotel for a place to sleep. They book an experience, a feeling, and a lifestyle.

The Wake-Up Call: When "Good Enough" Wasn't Enough

In the early days, our services were basic but functional: comfortable rooms, a simple breakfast, and standard amenities. Guests liked Mirabelle, but they didn't love it.

Then, one guest review caught my attention: "Nice hotel, friendly team. But nothing special. I could have stayed anywhere."

That hit me hard. If we weren't offering something unique, we were just another hotel. That's when I decided that Mirabelle wouldn't just provide accommodation; we would provide an unforgettable experience.

How We Made Our Products and Services Irresistible

To transform Mirabelle from "nice" to unforgettable, I focused on three key areas:

1. Make Every Product an Experience

- Are our rooms, food, and amenities special?
- Do they reflect our brand identity?
- Are guests excited to share their experience?

How we applied this at Mirabelle:

We redesigned our rooms with locally inspired décor and custom welcome gifts. Instead of a generic breakfast, we introduced a locally sourced, farm-to-table menu. We partnered with a nearby coffee roastery to offer guests exclusive blends. Every guest touchpoint became memorable, ensuring that our "product" stood out.

2. Offer Unique, High-Value Services

- Do we offer something guests can't get elsewhere?
- Are we anticipating their needs before they ask?
- Do we create moments that feel exclusive?

How we applied this at Mirabelle:

We launched "Sleep Well" packages—custom pillow menus, aromatherapy, and guided sleep meditations. We created exclusive guest experiences, like private city tours with local artists. We offered a personalized itinerary service, giving guests tailored recommendations. Now, guests weren't just booking a room—they were booking a curated experience.

3. Ensure a Strong Supply Chain for Products and Services

- Are our products consistently available and high-quality?
- Are services reliable, professional, and adaptable?
- Is our supply chain well-managed?

How we applied this at Mirabelle:

We built strong relationships with local suppliers to ensure fresh, high-quality food and amenities. We digitized inventory tracking to avoid shortages of guest essentials. We trained employees and teams in real-time service adjustments, allowing flexibility for unexpected guest needs. A well-managed supply chain ensured that our products and services were always delivered flawlessly.

Using the Right Instruments to Enhance Our Products and Services

Great experiences don't happen by chance; they are designed with the right management tools. Just as a cruise ship requires different navigation tools than a sailboat, a luxury boutique hotel like Mirabelle needed the right instruments to refine our products and services.

Structured Service Design: We developed a framework to ensure that every product and service aligned with Mirabelle's identity and guest expectations.

Testing New Offerings: Before launching any new feature, we followed a structured testing process (Plan-Do-Check-Act). We gathered guest feedback before making permanent changes.

Data-Driven Decision-Making: We used guest surveys and online reviews to refine our offerings, ensuring we adapted to trends in real time.

Knowledge Utilization: Our team had access to internal good practices, ensuring consistency in guest experience. And we encouraged everyone to update good practices whenever possible.

Technology for Seamless Service: We implemented a guest preference database, so returning guests received personalized service without needing to request it.

Risk Management for Service Continuity: We developed contingency plans to ensure uninterrupted service, whether due to supplier issues or unexpected guest demands.

Example: When one of our key suppliers (for high-end organic toiletries) suddenly closed, our risk plan allowed us to switch to an alternative supplier within 24 hours, ensuring that guests never noticed the disruption.

Using these instruments, Mirabelle wasn't just improving products and services—we were future-proofing them.

The Impact: How Our Upgraded Services Changed Everything

Guest satisfaction increased—our review scores went up because guests saw real value.

Repeat bookings doubled—guests returned not just for comfort but for the unique experience.

Word-of-mouth marketing grew—people started sharing their Mirabelle moments on social media.

One guest told me: "I've stayed in many boutique hotels, but this is the first one where I felt like every little detail was designed to make my stay special." That's when I knew—we weren't just running a hotel anymore; we were creating something people truly loved.

Final Lesson: Products and Services Define Your Brand

Service alone isn't enough—your offerings must be exceptional. Every detail should add value to the guest experience. Innovation keeps your business exciting and relevant.

At Mirabelle, we don't just provide a place to stay. We provide an experience people can't wait to return to.

Make Your Life Easier with Good Organization

In the early days of Mirabelle, I was juggling a million things at once: Managing bookings, handling guest requests, coordinating with suppliers, overseeing housekeeping, and training new employees. I was exhausted, overwhelmed, and constantly putting out fires. That's when I realized that success isn't about working harder, it's about organizing smarter.

A well-organized business doesn't just run smoother, it creates a better experience for everyone.

The Chaos Before Organization

One morning, a guest called to request an early breakfast at 6 AM. I assured them it wouldn't be a problem—except the kitchen team wasn't informed in time; the front desk assumed it was handled, so they didn't follow up. The guest arrived at the restaurant, and nothing was ready. The guest left frustrated, and I had to personally apologize. That's when I knew that without strong organization, even small mistakes become big problems.

I needed to align our structure with our processes; otherwise, Mirabelle would never run smoothly.

How We Built a Strong, Stress-Free Organization

To fix the chaos and make life easier for everyone, I focused on three key areas:

1. Align Structure with Processes

- Does our organization support our workflows—or make them harder?

- Are teams structured around processes instead of just hierarchy?
- Is there a clear flow of accountability?

How we applied this at Mirabelle:

We restructured departments so that teams were aligned with key guest experiences (check-in, housekeeping, dining) rather than isolated silos. We assigned clear process owners for every major guest touchpoint, so there was always someone accountable. We ensured leaders were process facilitators, not just managers helping their teams optimize efficiency.

Example: Before, housekeeping only took instructions from the front desk, causing delays. Now, they are directly connected to guest requests in real-time, eliminating miscommunication.

With this approach, our organization no longer slowed us down—it empowered us.

2. Streamline Communication and Role Clarity

- Do employees know exactly who is responsible for what?
- Are we avoiding miscommunication?
- Are our teams truly collaborating?

How we applied this at Mirabelle:

We implemented a centralized task management system so all teams (front desk, housekeeping, kitchen) had real-time updates. We created a daily briefing system—every morning, managers met for 10 minutes to review priorities. We introduced a shared digital logbook, so guest requests were never lost in miscommunication.

Now, when a guest made a request, everyone knew about it on time, every time.

3. Automate and Systematize for Efficiency

- Are we wasting time on repetitive tasks?
- Can technology help us work smarter?
- What tools can we use to simplify processes?

How we applied this at Mirabelle:

We automated guest check-ins and payments, reducing front desk workload by 40%. We used AI-driven inventory tracking, so we never ran out of essentials. We introduced self-service booking modifications, reducing call volumes and making it easier for guests.

Example: Before, all requests had to go through the front desk manually. Now, guests can modify their reservations digitally, and changes are automatically updated across all systems.

Instead of getting stuck in daily manual work, our team could focus on creating better guest experiences.

The Power of Organizational Structure in Business Success

I learned that a great organization isn't just about efficiency, it's about making life easier for everyone. After implementing structure, employees felt less stressed because they knew exactly what to do. Guest satisfaction improved because service became faster and more seamless, and operations became scalable. We could handle more guests without chaos.

One of my team members, Alex, told me: "Before, I felt like I was always firefighting. Now, I actually have time to focus on making guests happy instead of fixing internal issues." That's when I knew that organization wasn't just about making the hotel run better; it was about making life easier for everyone.

Learning from the Best: How Toyota Uses Structure to Support Processes

When I studied how world-class businesses organize themselves, I found that companies like Toyota don't just have great processes, they design their entire structure around those processes. When processes drive the organization, not the other way around: Roles are clearly defined to support key workflows, teams are organized by value streams, eliminating unnecessary layers of approval.

What We Learned from Toyota and Applied at Mirabelle:

Instead of rigid departmental silos, we structured teams around guest needs. We gave employees ownership over improving processes—just like Toyota's Kaizen method. We removed unnecessary bottlenecks, empowering employees to make quick decisions without needing constant managerial approval.

The result was a hotel that ran smoother, solved problems faster, and adapted more easily.

Final Lesson: Organization Is the Key to a Stress-Free Business

- A disorganized business leads to stress, mistakes, and poor guest experiences.
- Good organization creates smoother workflows, happier employees, and better service.
- When systems work well, everyone can focus on what truly matters—delivering excellence.

At Mirabelle, we don't just work harder, we work smarter because a well-organized business is a successful one.

Be Efficient with Good Project Management

When I first started Mirabelle, I was managing everything like a never-ending to-do list: Hiring employees, organizing guest services, managing suppliers, overseeing renovations, and running marketing campaigns. I was constantly busy but felt like I was getting nowhere. That's when I realized that being busy is not the same as being productive.

Success doesn't come from working harder; it comes from managing projects efficiently with clear goals, structured execution, and continuous improvement.

The Wake-Up Call: A Renovation Nightmare

One year, we planned a guest room renovation project. It should have been simple, but timelines weren't clearly set, so contractors delayed work; suppliers weren't coordinated, so furniture arrived late; and departments weren't aligned, so the front desk team didn't know which rooms were unavailable.

The result was guests were checked into rooms that weren't ready, the project cost more due to delays and last-minute fixes, and our reputation took a hit with frustrated guests.

That's when I knew that if I didn't master project management, Mirabelle would never grow efficiently. I needed a structured approach to ensure that every project ran on time, within budget, and without chaos.

Applying the STEPS 1-5 Framework to Project Management

I learned that successful project management follows a structured approach. Whether you're running a hotel renovation or a multimillion-dollar construction project, the same fundamental STEPS apply.

STEP 1: Define an Attractive Success Picture

Before starting any project, define a clear and compelling vision that excites everyone involved.

How we applied this at Mirabelle:

Instead of just saying "Let's renovate some rooms", we framed it as: "By the end of this project, we will create a premium boutique hotel experience that exceeds guest expectations and positions Mirabelle as a top-tier destination."

This success picture aligned everyone, from contractors to front desk team, around a shared goal.

STEP 2: Involve Key Interest Groups and Assess Risks

Before planning, involve all interest groups related to the project, understand their expectations, and identify potential risks early.

How we applied this at Mirabelle:

We consulted employees from housekeeping, front desk, and maintenance to understand operational pain points. We analyzed guest feedback to ensure our renovations addressed real customer needs. We conducted a risk assessment—identifying potential delays, supply chain disruptions, and guest inconveniences.

The result was that instead of just making rooms "look nicer", our project addressed real guest pain points, such as outdated lighting, noise control, and lack of modern amenities.

STEP 3: Develop a Balanced and Risk-Tested Project Plan

A good project plan isn't just about timelines, it balances success with performance, feasibility, and flexibility.

How we applied this at Mirabelle:

We set clear success goals, e.g., "Complete room renovations in 6 weeks without guest disruptions." We defined measurable performance targets such as reducing check-in issues by 30%. We balanced efficiency with guest experience, and we staggered renovations so that guests were never disturbed. We built in flexibility. We had contingency plans for supply chain issues and contractor delays.

The result was that we avoided guest complaints and completed the project without shutting down operations.

STEP 4: Ensure Smooth Implementation and Milestone Control

A project is only as strong as the people and tools behind it.

How we applied this at Mirabelle:

We hired the right suppliers and contractors prioritizing reliability over cost-cutting. We used project management tools to track progress, assign tasks, and avoid delays. We held milestone reviews at key points ensuring progress was on track and risks were addressed early. We regularly checked project success probability, adjusting the plan as needed instead of sticking to failing approaches.

A strong plan means nothing if execution fails. This step ensures smooth implementation.

STEP 5: Harvest Project Success and Continuous Improvement

Once a project ends, analyze its success and capture lessons for future improvements.

How we applied this at Mirabelle:

We conducted a post-project review seeing what worked, what didn't, and how to improve. We used guest feedback surveys to measure satisfaction with the new rooms. We documented best practices to ensure the next project ran even smoother.

The result was that each new project became more structured, efficient, and impactful than the last.

The Power of Good Project Management in Business Growth

Once we applied structured project management, everything changed: Projects finished faster and with fewer mistakes, costs were reduced because of better planning, employees felt less overwhelmed because responsibilities were clear, and guests experienced seamless service, even during renovations.

One of my managers, David, told me: "Before, projects felt chaotic. Now, we know exactly what needs to be done and when. It's like running a well-planned event every time." That's when I knew that good project management wasn't just about efficiency; it was about making business growth stress-free and predictable.

Learning from the Best: How Other Companies Master Project Management

When I studied how global companies execute complex projects, I found that industry leaders like Siemens follow structured project methodologies to ensure flawless execution.

Siemens Energy designs and builds power plants, using detailed milestones and risk mitigation plans.

SAP delivers enterprise software through custom implementation projects.

Hyundai Heavy Industries builds massive ships by treating each delivery as a structured project.

Disney treats every movie production as a highly managed project with clear goals and timelines.

What We Learned from Other Companies and Applied at Mirabelle

We created clear milestones and deliverables ensuring progress is measured at every step. We began strict risk assessments identifying potential delays before they happen. We defined project roles, so every team member knows their responsibilities.

By applying these principles, Mirabelle started executing projects like a world-class business.

Final Lesson: Great Businesses Run on Great Project Management

- Without planning, even the best ideas fail.
- Clear milestones and accountability prevent chaos.
- Continuous improvement makes every project smoother than the last.

At Mirabelle, we don't just take on projects, we execute them like a high-performing organization.

Use Relevant Data and Information

When I first started Mirabelle, I made decisions based on intuition and experience. I thought I knew what guests wanted. I guessed which services were most profitable, and I assumed I understood employee satisfaction. But I quickly realized a business that runs on assumptions is a business at risk.

Successful organizations don't guess. They analyze, measure, and act based on facts. That's when I made a commitment: Mirabelle would always use data and information to guide our growth.

The Wake-Up Call: When Gut Instinct Failed

One season, I noticed that our bar revenue was lower than expected. I assumed that guests weren't interested in the bar. The menu needed more variety, and that we should reduce investment in bar services.

Before making changes, I decided to analyze actual data.

I found that bar sales weren't dropping because guests didn't like it; sales were dropping because guests were spending more time in their rooms and on the terrace where they weren't being served drinks.

The real issue wasn't the bar, it was accessibility. Instead of changing the menu, we added mobile ordering from guest rooms and the terrace, trained employees to recommend signature drinks, and launched a "Happy Hour on the Terrace" promotion. Bar revenue increased by 35% in three months. That's when I realized that data gives you answers that intuition alone never will.

How We Started Using Data for Smarter Decisions

To run Mirabelle more effectively using data, I focused on three key areas:

1. Guest Preferences and Behavior

- What do guests love the most?
- What services do they use the least?
- How can we personalize their experience?

How we applied this at Mirabelle:

We used guest feedback surveys to identify what truly mattered. We tracked booking patterns not just who stayed, but when, why, and how often. We used AI-powered recommendations to offer personalized experiences (e.g., repeat guests received room preferences automatically).

The result was higher guest satisfaction and a 20% increase in repeat bookings.

2. Employee Productivity and Satisfaction

- Are employees engaged and motivated?
- What tasks take up the most time?
- Are we optimizing employment levels?

How we applied this at Mirabelle:

We collected anonymous employee feedback every quarter to identify stress points. We used shift performance data to reduce scheduling inefficiencies. We introduced automated task tracking, reducing time wasted on unnecessary tasks.

The result was happier employees, lower turnover, and a 15% improvement in service efficiency.

3. Financial and Operational Insights

- Which services are the most profitable?
- Where are we losing money?
- How can we optimize costs?

How we applied this at Mirabelle:

We tracked cost per guest per night to find areas for optimization. We analyzed return on investment (ROI) for all promotions, only keeping those that worked. We used dynamic pricing models to adjust rates based on demand, increasing revenue.

The result was reduced operational costs by 12% while improving overall profitability.

The Impact: How Data Transformed Mirabelle

Decisions became smarter and faster, guest experiences became more personalized, costs were optimized without sacrificing quality, and employees felt more valued and empowered. One guest told me: "I love how Mirabelle remembers my preferences—every time I return, it feels even more personalized." That's when I knew data wasn't just about numbers; it was about creating a better experience for everyone.

Final Lesson: Data Is the Key to Smart Growth

- Assumptions lead to mistakes—data leads to accuracy.
- The right information helps improve guest satisfaction, employee engagement, and financial performance.
- Data-driven decisions aren't just smarter; they make growth scalable.

At Mirabelle, we don't guess; we use data to drive success because the best decisions are backed by real insights.

Apply Own and Others' Knowledge in a Useful Way

When I first started Mirabelle, I thought I had to figure out everything on my own. I believed that, as the owner, I needed to have all the answers, make every key decision myself, and rely on my own experience to solve problems. But I quickly realized something: the smartest leaders aren't the ones who know everything, they're the ones who know how to use knowledge effectively. Success isn't just about what I know; it's about combining my knowledge with the expertise of my team, mentors, and industry insights.

The Wake-Up Call: When My Own Knowledge Wasn't Enough

Early on, I struggled with optimizing revenue. I tried adjusting room prices based on seasons, offering last-minute discounts, and running promotions for returning guests. But revenue growth was slow, and I couldn't figure out why. Then, I had a conversation with a hotel revenue expert, who asked me: "Are you using a dynamic pricing model based on demand, events, and competitor pricing?"

I wasn't. I had been relying on my own experience instead of learning from someone who specialized in hotel revenue strategies. We implemented a dynamic pricing system, and within three months, revenue increased by 18% with no additional marketing costs. That's when I learned success isn't just about what I know. It's about learning from the right people and applying that knowledge effectively.

How I Started Using Knowledge More Effectively

To make sure we, at Mirabelle, were applying knowledge in a useful way, I focused on three key areas:

1. Learn from Experts and Industry Best Practices

- Who has already solved the problems I'm facing?
- What strategies are other successful businesses using?
- How can I apply those insights to Mirabelle?

How we applied this at Mirabelle:

We joined hospitality business forums to stay updated on industry trends, we consulted with hotel tech experts to optimize our online booking system, and we studied successful boutique hotels to understand what made them stand out.

The result was that we avoided common mistakes and implemented proven strategies faster.

2. Leverage the Knowledge of My Team

- Are we using the expertise of our employees?

- Do we encourage team members to share their insights?
- How do we apply internal knowledge to improve operations?

How we applied this at Mirabelle:

We launched a "Team Knowledge Hub", where employees could suggest improvements based on their experience; we encouraged department heads to lead knowledge-sharing sessions, so employees could learn from each other; and we tested and implemented employee ideas—like a front desk manager's suggestion to offer personalized check-ins, which increased guest satisfaction.

The result was that employees felt valued, engaged, and invested in the hotel's success.

3. Document and Systematize Knowledge for Continuous Improvement

- Are we keeping track of what works and what doesn't?
- Do we have a system for sharing and applying knowledge?
- How can we improve and evolve over time?

How we applied this at Mirabelle:

We created SOPs (Standard Operating Procedures) for guest interactions, housekeeping, and event management; we built a digital knowledge library, where all best practices, guest insights, and team suggestions were stored; and we held monthly review meetings to evaluate what was working and what needed improvement.

The result was that new employees learned faster and efficiency increased across all departments.

The Impact: How Applying Knowledge Transformed Mirabelle

When we applied knowledge, problems were solved faster because we weren't reinventing the wheel; innovation increased because we combined industry knowledge with employee creativity; and decision-making improved because we had access to real insights, not just guesses. One of my senior employees, Mark, told me: "The difference between this hotel and others is that ideas don't just stay as ideas. Here, if something works, it becomes part of how we do things." That's when I knew that knowledge is only valuable when it's applied.

Final Lesson: Knowledge is Power—But Only If You Use It

- The best businesses don't rely only on what the owner knows— they use collective knowledge.
- Learning from experts and employees helps avoid mistakes and improve efficiency.
- Documenting and applying knowledge makes success scalable and repeatable.

At Mirabelle, we don't just collect information; we apply it, share it, and use it to grow because smart knowledge management leads to smarter success.

Document Relevant Matters Appropriately

When I first started Mirabelle, I underestimated the importance of proper documentation.

I believed that as long as I had a great team, clear goals, strong daily operations, things would run smoothly. But then, reality hit. Without proper documentation, important details get lost, miscommunication happens, and mistakes repeat themselves. A well-documented business isn't just organized; it's efficient, scalable, and protected.

The Wake-Up Call: A Guest Compensation Disaster

One evening, a guest named Emma had an issue with her room's air-conditioning. We moved her to another room and offered a complimentary meal as an apology.

The next morning, the front desk had no record of the meal being free, and the guest was charged for it at checkout. She was frustrated. It felt like a broken promise. This situation could have easily been avoided with better documentation. That's when I realized: if something isn't written down, it doesn't exist.

How We Built a Strong Documentation System

To ensure that Mirabelle operated efficiently, I focused on three key documentation areas:

1. Operational Documentation: Ensure Consistency and Clarity

- Are tasks and procedures clearly documented?
- Can new employees learn quickly from written processes?
- Do all team members have access to the same information?

How we applied this at Mirabelle:

We created Standard Operating Procedures (SOPs) for everything like housekeeping, front desk, customer service, and crisis handling. We introduced daily shift logs where employees recorded key issues, VIP requests, and special instructions. We developed a hotel manual, ensuring consistency in guest experience.

The result was that new employees learned 50% faster, and errors decreased significantly.

2. Guest Interaction Documentation: Avoid Miscommunication

- Are guest requests and special situations properly recorded?
- Do all departments have access to the same guest information?
- Can we track guest preferences for a personalized experience?

How we applied this at Mirabelle:

We integrated a shared guest profile system tracking preferences, special requests, and past issues. We implemented a guest incident log, ensuring that all departments knew about any service recovery efforts, and we created a compensation tracking system to prevent repeat mistakes like Emma's.

The result was that guest satisfaction improved and personalized service became our competitive advantage.

3. Legal and Financial Documentation: Protect the Business

- Are contracts, policies, and compliance records up-to-date?
- Are financial records easily accessible and well-organized?
- Do we have documentation for regulatory inspections and audits?

How we applied this at Mirabelle:

We digitized all contracts and agreements ensuring easy access and security; maintained detailed financial records for budgeting and investor transparency; and created a regulatory compliance checklist, ensuring that we were always audit-ready.

The result was that we avoided legal risks, improved financial planning, and stayed compliant.

The Impact: How Proper Documentation Transformed Mirabelle

With good documentation, there was no more lost information; employees had instant access to essential details. There was faster problem resolution because past issues were well-documented, and we improved guest trust because we delivered consistent, error-free service. One returning guest, after receiving their preferred breakfast exactly how they liked it, told me: "I don't know how you do it, but every time I come back, it feels like you remember everything about me!" That's when I knew good documentation wasn't just about efficiency; it was about creating a better experience.

Final Lesson: What Gets Documented, Gets Done

- A well-documented business eliminates confusion and mistakes.
- Guest interactions should always be tracked for personalized service.
- Legal, financial, and compliance records protect the business.
- Proper documentation makes growth and scaling easier.

At Mirabelle, we don't rely on memory; we document, track, and improve because what gets written down, gets done right.

Use Helpful (Future) Technologies

When I started Mirabelle, I believed that hospitality was about people, not technology. But I quickly realized that technology doesn't replace hospitality; it enhances it. The right technologies don't just make operations smoother, they improve guest experiences, boost efficiency, and future-proof the business. That's when I made a commitment that Mirabelle would stay ahead by using smart, future-ready technology.

The Wake-Up Call: When Manual Systems Failed Us

One night, during peak season, our front desk was overwhelmed with check-ins. Guests had to wait 15+ minutes just to get their room keys; our reservation system crashed, delaying check-ins further; and a guest got the wrong room because of a manual entry mistake. I saw the frustration on our guests' faces. That night, I realized that if we didn't embrace technology, we'd fall behind.

How We Integrated Smart Technologies

To future-proof Mirabelle, I focused on three key areas of tech innovation:

1. Smart Guest Experience Technology

- Can guests check in and out seamlessly?
- Are we personalizing their stay using data?
- Do they have more control over their experience?

How we applied this at Mirabelle:

We began to use mobile check-in and digital room keys, reducing front desk wait times by 70%; used AI-powered chatbots for 24/7 guest support and booking inquiries; and implemented smart room controls, allowing guests to adjust lighting, temperature, and music via an app.

The result was that guests felt more in control, and service became faster and more personalized.

2. Operational Efficiency and Automation

- Can technology reduce employee workload?
- Are we automating repetitive tasks?
- Are we optimizing resources to cut costs?

How we applied this at Mirabelle:

We began using AI-driven housekeeping scheduling, reducing turnaround times by 30%. We automated inventory management, preventing stock shortages; we implemented self-service kiosks, allowing guests to access concierge services faster.

The result was that employees spent less time on repetitive tasks and more time creating great guest experiences.

3. Data and Predictive Technologies

- Are we making smart, data-driven decisions?
- Can we predict guest preferences and behavior?
- How can we use AI to stay ahead of trends?

How we applied this at Mirabelle:

We implemented AI-powered dynamic pricing, adjusting room rates based on demand in real time. We started guest preference tracking, offering customized services based on past stays; we implemented predictive analytics, forecasting occupancy rates and seasonal trends.

The result was higher revenue, better guest personalization, and smarter business planning.

The Impact: How Tech Transformed Mirabelle

Check-in times dropped from 15 minutes to under 2 minutes; housekeeping became 30% more efficient, reducing operational costs; and guest satisfaction scores increased, thanks to seamless service. One returning guest told me: "I love how I can check in with my phone, unlock my room without a key, and control everything with one app. It's the perfect mix of luxury and convenience!" That's when I knew embracing future technology wasn't just a business move; it was the key to staying ahead.

Beyond Technology: Other Key Resources for Success

At Mirabelle, technology transformed the way we operated, but I soon realized that technology alone isn't enough. A successful business also needs the right financial, physical, and intellectual resources to sustain long-term growth.

That's when I made sure that Mirabelle was investing in the right foundational resources.

Financial Resources: We optimized our budget and cash flow management to fund new initiatives—like upgrading our technology and expanding guest services.

Physical Resources: We renovated our facilities to ensure a luxurious, comfortable experience while investing in sustainable solutions to reduce energy consumption.

Intellectual Resources: We protected our brand reputation and invested in employee training programs to ensure that knowledge was shared and retained across the team.

The result was that by balancing technology with strong financial, physical, and intellectual resources, Mirabelle became resilient, future-ready, and positioned for sustainable growth.

Final Lesson: Smart Technology = Smarter Business

- Future-ready hotels use technology to enhance—not replace—hospitality.
- Automation boosts efficiency, cuts costs, and improves guest satisfaction.
- Data-driven decisions lead to smarter growth and long-term success.
- A well-resourced business is a resilient business.

At Mirabelle, we don't fear the future; we embrace technology and smart resource management to create a seamless, unforgettable guest experience.

Handle Important Operational Risks with Care

Running Mirabelle taught me a valuable lesson early on: A great business isn't just about delivering exceptional service—it's about managing risks before they become disasters. I used to believe that as long as things were running smoothly, everything was fine. But then I learned the hard way that ignoring operational risks doesn't make them go away—it makes them harder to control when they happen. That's when I made a commitment: Mirabelle would prioritize risk management, ensuring that every challenge was anticipated and handled with care.

The Wake-Up Call: A Water Leak That Became a PR Nightmare

One morning, our housekeeping team discovered a small water leak in one of the guest bathrooms. Since it didn't seem urgent, we planned to fix it the next day. But by that evening the leak had spread to the room below, a guest complained about water dripping from their ceiling, soaking their luggage, and they took to social media, posting about their "ruined vacation" and our slow response.

What started as a minor maintenance issue turned into a PR and reputation crisis. That's when I realized that operational risks, no matter how small, must be handled immediately and with a clear process.

How We Built a Risk-Handling Framework

After that experience, I developed a risk management system focused on the five STEPS:

STEP 1: Identify Risks

- What could go wrong in daily operations?
- Which risks are urgent and which can be managed over time?
- Are we tracking recurring issues?

How we applied this at Mirabelle:

We created a risk checklist covering maintenance, safety, guest services, and technology. We defined risk categories—minor (can wait), moderate (needs attention soon), and critical (must be handled immediately), and we encouraged all employees to report even small risks, preventing them from escalating.

The result was that problems were identified early, reducing surprises and emergency fixes.

STEP 2: Assess Risks

- How likely is the risk to occur?
- What is the potential impact on guest experience, operations, or costs?
- Are there trends in past incidents that can help predict future risks?

How we applied this at Mirabelle:

We tracked past guest complaints to identify recurring maintenance issues, used data from previous emergencies to assess response times and weak points, and implemented a probability and impact matrix to prioritize risks effectively.

The result was that we stopped reacting blindly and started preparing strategically.

STEP 3: Define Countermeasures

- What can we do to prevent or minimize these risks?
- How can we ensure that we're always prepared?

How we applied this at Mirabelle:

We implemented a preventive maintenance plan, so repairs happened before issues escalated; trained employees on quick response actions for common risks like plumbing issues, power failures, and fire alarms; and installed a real-time risk reporting system, so every issue was logged and assigned immediately.

The result was that we minimized disruptions and improved operational stability.

STEP 4: Prepare Crisis and Emergency Management

- Do employees know exactly what to do when things go wrong?
- Do we have clear emergency response protocols?

How we applied this at Mirabelle:

We introduced a "handle it now" policy where any issue affecting guests had to be addressed immediately, no delays. We conducted emergency response drills, ensuring all employees knew how to handle situations like evacuations, security threats, or system failures, and we created a guest communication protocol, so guests were informed transparently in case of disruptions.

The result was that employees felt confident and prepared, and guests trusted our ability to handle issues professionally.

STEP 5: Ensure Business Continuity

- How do we recover quickly after a risk event?

- How do we minimize downtime and keep operations running smoothly?

How we applied this at Mirabelle:

We developed a business continuity plan, so we had backup solutions for critical operations; partnered with emergency service providers, ensuring immediate support in case of urgent incidents; and created an incident review system, where we analyzed every major issue and improved our response plans.

The result was that we were no longer caught off-guard and were always prepared for the unexpected.

The Impact: How Risk Management Strengthened Mirabelle

With a risk management strategy, we had fewer service disruptions because problems were handled proactively, higher guest trust because issues were addressed before they escalated, and stronger brand reputation because we consistently delivered a seamless experience. One guest, who experienced a minor issue that was resolved within minutes, told me: "I've never seen a hotel handle a problem so quickly and professionally. That's why I'll keep coming back." That's when I knew that great hospitality isn't about avoiding problems; it's about how well you handle them.

Final Lesson: Proactive Risk Management Creates a Resilient Business

- Small risks can become big problems if ignored.
- A structured risk management system prevents chaos.
- Empowering employees to act fast improves guest trust.
- Continuous improvement keeps the business ahead of potential threats.

At Mirabelle, we don't just react to problems; we anticipate, prevent, and manage them with care—because that's what true excellence requires.

Always Act Sustainably

When I first opened Mirabelle, sustainability wasn't my top priority. I focused on guest experience, service quality, and operational efficiency But then I started noticing something: Modern travelers care about sustainability, and they expect businesses to care too. Sustainability isn't just an ethical choice—it's a business necessity, and can be turned into a competitive advantage. That's when I realized that Mirabelle couldn't just be a great hotel; it had to be a responsible one too.

The Wake-Up Call: When Guests Started Asking Questions

One day, a guest approached me at checkout and asked: "I love this hotel, but do you use eco-friendly products? I try to stay at places that are committed to sustainability." I didn't have a clear answer. I realized we were using single-use plastics for toiletries, our energy consumption was higher than it needed to be, and we weren't actively supporting the local environment or community. That was the moment I knew that sustainability couldn't be an afterthought—it had to be part of our identity.

How We Built a Sustainable Business Model

To make Mirabelle truly sustainable, I focused on three key areas, aligned with the three ESG pillars:

1. Ensure Sustainable Environmental Responsibility (E)

- Are we minimizing plastic and unnecessary waste?
- Can we reduce water and energy use?
- Are we using sustainable materials?

How we applied this at Mirabelle:

We reduced waste by switching to biodegradable and refillable toiletries, installed LED lighting and motion-sensor energy-saving systems, and introduced water conservation measures, including low-flow showers and towel-reuse programs.

The result was that guests appreciated the effort, and utility costs dropped by 25%.

2. Ensure Sustainable Social Responsibility (S)

- Are we reducing our carbon footprint by sourcing nearby?
- Are we supporting local farmers, artisans, and businesses?
- Are we reinvesting in our community?

How we applied this at Mirabelle:

We partnered with local farmers for fresh, organic food; decorated the hotel with art from local artists, showcasing regional talent; and started a guest donation initiative, allowing guests to contribute to local sustainability projects.

The result was that guests loved the authentic, eco-conscious experience, and we built strong community relationships.

3. Ensure Sustainable Governance (G)

- Are we making sustainability part of the guest experience?
- Are we transparent about our eco-friendly efforts?
- Are we inspiring guests to be more sustainable, too?

How we applied this at Mirabelle:

We created a "Green Stay" program—offering discounts for guests who chose eco-friendly options (e.g., skipping daily room cleaning); hosted sustainability workshops, like zero-waste cooking classes and eco-friendly travel tips; and included sustainability reports in guest welcome kits, showing our commitment to the environment.

The result was that guests became more engaged with our sustainability mission, and participation in our eco-programs grew by 40%.

The Impact: How Sustainability Made Mirabelle Stronger

With sustainability measures, eco-conscious travelers became loyal guests, operational costs dropped due to reduced waste and energy use, and we became a leader in sustainable hospitality, attracting positive media attention. One guest told me: "I love that Mirabelle doesn't just talk about sustainability—you actually live it. That's why I choose to stay here." That's when I knew acting sustainably wasn't just good for the planet; it was great for business too.

Final Lesson: Sustainability Is the Future of Business

- Guests expect businesses to be environmentally responsible.
- Sustainability reduces costs, improves reputation, and builds customer loyalty.
- The best businesses don't just react to trends—they lead the way in sustainability.

At Mirabelle, we don't just care about today; we act sustainably to create a better future—for our guests, our community, and our planet.

Chapter Five

Secure Sustainable Success (STEP 5)

Success is more than just a destination; it's a journey. True success happens when all your interest groups are satisfied—this is the vision for excellence. General satisfaction creates success for your organization, filling you with pride and a sense of accomplishment.

But success is not the finish line. It's a stepping stone for your continuous improvement. That's why the KAIZUNO method emphasizes that feedback from your interest groups is very important, because it shows you exactly where you can further improve as an organization.

Measure the Satisfaction of Interest Groups

To know how satisfied your interest groups really are, you need to measure their satisfaction. Due to the different nature of your relationships with different interest groups, there is no standard way to measure satisfaction. Rather, approaches and instruments need to be adapted to match the specific relationship requirements. What may work for customers, might not work for people or key decision-makers. Ways that work for large organizations may not work for small- or medium-size companies. Some methods are culture-specific. Some work better in a digital version, others might not.

As organizations develop, the portfolio of ways to collect expectations from interest groups has to be adapted and optimized to match changes in relationships. These adjustments must be made very carefully so as not to damage relationships with interest groups.

Although benchmarking of approaches, instruments, and tools may help in some cases, it can be dangerous to copy/paste good practices of other organizations. Here is an example: A large manufacturing plant adopts a digital survey methodology as a benchmarking result in the industry sector. They use it for their 630 workers, who don't have personal laptops or business smartphones. To respond to the digital survey on the intranet, workers need to use one of the 10 digital terminals in production. Since people don't like that, and the response rate of the survey is very low.

Many organizations use formal surveys to collect feedback from customers, people, and suppliers and partners. Because the feedback in these surveys is typically collected anonymously, responses can be analyzed easily with statistical methods to find out what that interest group likes or dislikes.

One disadvantage of anonymous surveys is that individual feedback is not collected. Some additional open questions can help gather individual feedback on specific critical issues. Individual feedback is often very valuable, but time-consuming to evaluate. In addition, it must be ensured that no conclusions can be drawn about individual persons.

The willingness to give honest feedback in surveys depends very much on the culture of your organization, and specifically on your desire to improve. A key factor is the interest group's experience with previous surveys. Was critical feedback really accepted and used for improvements, or was it somewhat ignored?

Satisfy Your Interest Groups

If you have consistently applied STEPS 1 through 4, measurements will clearly demonstrate improved satisfaction of your interest groups. You will probably not have achieved balanced satisfaction across all interest groups— since this is the vision for excellence—but you will certainly have increased the satisfaction of at least some interest groups. Comparisons with internal satisfaction targets and external benchmarks can show where the gaps are.

Although it may sound pretty incredible, there are actually many organizations that do not make any further use of these findings. Especially in cases where the measured satisfaction is significantly below expectations, no further action is often taken. Sometimes, the results of satisfaction measurements are kept confidential and not even communicated. To understand this strange behavior, a comparison with our private lives helps: we sometimes ignore feedback that we receive about our behavior from a family member. You have certainly experienced the consequences of this ignorance for yourself.

Neglecting feedback from interest groups can have significant negative consequences and seriously jeopardize your success. Here are some examples.

Environmental groups and regulators flagged discrepancies in *Volkswagen's* emissions data. Rather than addressing the issues early on, the company attempted to cover up the manipulation of emissions tests. Once exposed, VW faced billions in fines, massive reputational damage, and a sharp decline in customer trust globally.

Kodak ignored the shift toward digital photography, even as customers expressed interest in digital solutions. This ignorance allowed competitors to capture the market, leading to Kodak's financial struggles and eventual bankruptcy.

The only legitimization to obtain feedback from interest groups should be your honest desire to derive and implement improvements from the findings. In this spirit, every professionally conducted survey will help to further improve relations with your interest groups, their satisfaction, and thus the success of your organization.

Use Feedback to Increase Satisfaction

Every interaction with your interest groups to measure their satisfaction contains their hidden expectation that you will use their feedback to make improvements for their benefit. This is a natural expectation that you know from your private interactions. But although this expectation exists, it is often not openly expressed. If you disappoint this expectation, your relationship with that interest group might deteriorate and you may wish you had never asked for feedback.

Below is a **best practice survey process** that ensures that those expectations are honored. If you use this approach, there is a very high probability that your survey will significantly improve your relationship with your interest groups, thus their satisfaction and eventually your success.

Ensure that Questions Are Relevant

To ensure that your interest group representatives like your survey and are motivated to provide their feedback, make sure your questions are relevant for them. Otherwise, your interest groups do not feel respected and will not respond, since they consider your survey a waste of time. A questionnaire full of irrelevant questions (from the perspective of your interest group) can seriously deteriorate your relationship.

A simple way to find out which topics are relevant and interesting for your interest group is to ask them, e.g., by discussing your draft questionnaire in an informal meeting over a meal. They will immediately tell you which questions they consider relevant and which not. You may still decide to keep some questions that are relevant only for you, but be aware of the potential consequences.

Note: Some organizations hesitate changing their questionnaires since they want to compare feedback results from one survey to the next. Also, some assessment rules require organizations to demonstrate positive trends over many years. But think twice: What is the major reason for conducting a survey? You want to learn from feedback where you can improve, and implement improvements to optimize relationships and satisfaction of your interest groups. Compared with this success goal, tracking improvements over several years as a trend may be an interesting additional information, but not so important.

Relevance and Importance

Since your interest group representatives are human beings and the world is changing, relevance will change over time. Topics that were highly relevant for your interest group last year may be less relevant today. To track changes in interest group's relevance of topics, use this simple approach: for every question you ask, don't just ask the perception of your interest group on this topic (e.g., very satisfied or less satisfied). Add an additional column where you ask "How important is this topic for you?" on a scale from "very important" to "less important".

With this additional information, you can analyze your survey results in two dimensions: satisfaction versus importance, both from their point of view. This will make it easier to plan your actions, since dissatisfaction with less important aspects is less serious than dissatisfaction with very important aspects. If you use these two dimensions in your ensuing surveys, you can track changes in importance, which will allow you to adapt your questionnaire next time. This ensures that you are always up-to-date with your interest group's preferences, which is the best possible basis for your decisions.

Collect Feedback and Make Promises

The methods and media you use to collect feedback must fit your individual relationships with every interest group. While a survey via your website may be appropriate for your customers, an old-fashioned paper-based questionnaire may be adequate for your employees. If interest groups are asked to use a method or media that they do not like, they will not take the time to answer your questions.

Always distribute your survey together with a friendly, signed letter from your highest-ranking officer or customer manager, which includes a "thank you" and a commitment: You promise to analyze all feedback within the shortest possible time and communicate the resulting improvement plans. The best practice time for these activities is 4 weeks—for a very large organization.

Make sure you can keep your promise exactly. Therefore, before even sending out your survey, you should agree on the whole survey process, making sure leaders are committed and people, talent, and resources are available to manage the selected improvement projects.

It may sound strange, but keeping your promises is more important for the relationship with your interest groups than the successful implementation of your improvements. By keeping your promise, you strengthen trust in your organization. If you do not succeed in implementing all improvement projects as planned, and you can justify this well, you will be forgiven.

Only few organizations know that the survey process itself is the most critical aspect of a survey. Many organizations keep damaging good interest group relations by making fundamental mistakes with the survey process.

Analyze Results, Share and Implement Improvements, Ensure Benefit

Analyze feedback, decide on a handful of improvement projects, and send out your letter not one day later as promised. Your letter includes a list of improvement projects and another promise: to keep your interest group informed about the progress of your projects. Every positive update will further increase their trust in you.

Do not select too many and too large projects, since you want to demonstrate tangible benefit for your interest group within a couple of months—in any case, well before the next survey. If you wait too long, your interest groups will have forgotten that you asked them in the first place.

You can apply this survey process as a perfect closed loop: collect feedback, turn it into improvements, then ask again for feedback. Every loop has two success factors: you show to your interest group that you are reliable by keeping your promises, and you create benefit for them. This increases the satisfaction of your interest group with every loop.

Harvest the Fruits of Your Success

Every satisfied interest group will increase the likelihood of your successes.

Financial Success:

- Increased revenue and profit: Loyal customers, productive employees, and strong partnerships lead to higher sales and cost efficiency.
- Attracting investments: Satisfied interest groups and a good reputation attract investors who see your organization as low-risk and high-potential.
- Sustainable growth: Long-term financial stability due to consistent demand and operational efficiency.

Success Through Satisfied Customers:

- High customer satisfaction and loyalty: Meeting or exceeding customer expectations ensures repeat business and positive referrals.

- Market leadership: Becoming a preferred brand in the market due to strong customer trust and advocacy.

- Innovation: Satisfied customers provide valuable feedback that drives product or service improvements.

Success Through Engaged Employees:

- High employee engagement and productivity: Happy and motivated employees contribute more effectively to the organization.

- Talent attraction and retention: Satisfied employees promote the company as a great place to work, attracting top talent.

- Positive workplace culture: A strong, collaborative culture that enhances creativity and innovation.

Success Through Satisfied Partners and Suppliers:

- Stronger relationships: Satisfied partners and suppliers lead to better collaboration and supply chain efficiency.

- Cost savings and quality improvements: Stable partnerships ensure consistent quality and competitive pricing.

- Shared innovation: Strong partnerships foster co-creation of innovative solutions.

Success Through Society:

- Reputation and brand value: Positive societal impact enhances the organization's reputation and builds trust with the public.

- Sustainability Leadership: Reducing environmental impact earns recognition as an environmentally responsible organization.

- Cost Savings: Energy efficiency, waste reduction and resource optimization lower operational costs.

Success Through Satisfied Key Decision-Makers:

- Strategic alignment: Satisfied decision-makers (e.g., boards, investors, regulators) ensure alignment with long-term business goals.

- Support for innovation and growth: Satisfied decision-makers are more willing to approve new investments and initiatives.

- Risk mitigation: Satisfied shareholders reduce resistance to changes and foster smoother implementation of ambitious plans.

Be Proud of Your Success

If you are successful, you have every reason to be proud. Celebrating success together with selected interest groups is a way to recognize everyone who actively supported and contributed to your success journey.

What can you do if you want external confirmation and recognition for your success?

You can compare your success against benchmarks in various dimensions like financial, market share, quality, sustainability. External consultants can help find suitable benchmarks. For instance, third-party survey benchmarks can validate employee satisfaction and organizational culture.

Some customers provide comparison lists of their best suppliers, but mostly in neutral form. Nevertheless, you can clearly see where you stand in comparison with other suppliers.

There are many institutions around the world that carry out assessments to measure the success of organizations and compare it with benchmarks. These comparisons relate to specific aspects (e.g., leadership, production, sustainability) or to the entire organization.

Excellence award institutions compare your success with a hypothetical "perfect" organization that completely satisfies all interest groups at the same time. Depending on your success level, you may get recognitions and even global awards that you can use for marketing.

To share your success story beyond your own sphere of influence, you can collaborate with media outlets who may share your success story with respected publications.

Secure Your Existence in the Future

The consistent application of KAIZUNO will help you secure your existence in the future.

Success isn't a one-time event—it's a continuous journey. KAIZUNO ensures that organizations not only achieve success but **sustain it over time** by measuring satisfaction, adapting to new challenges, and continuously improving.

Maya Dani had built something great—but could she make it last? Let's return to her story with her hotel and explore how she ensured long-term success.

Secure Sustainable Success (STEP 5) - Application

Measure the Satisfaction of Interest Groups

When I first started Mirabelle, I assumed that as long as guests kept coming back, we were doing well. But then I realized that if you don't measure satisfaction, you can't improve it. Success isn't just about offering great service; it's about ensuring that every interest group is truly satisfied. That's when I made a commitment: Mirabelle wouldn't just assume—we would measure, analyze, and continuously improve.

The Wake-Up Call: When Guests Left Without Returning

One month, I noticed that our repeat guest rate had dropped. I checked reviews, and everything seemed fine, so I asked myself: *What if there's a problem we're not seeing?* That's when I started actively measuring satisfaction.

I found that guests weren't unhappy—but they also weren't excited, employees felt overworked during peak seasons, and suppliers wanted better communication for long-term planning. These were things I would have never known without asking the right questions.

That's when I realized that to improve, we first need to understand what's working—and what's not.

How We Measured Satisfaction Across All Interest Groups

To make Mirabelle better, I focused on three key groups:

1. Guest Satisfaction: Understand Their Experience

- Are guests truly happy with their stay?
- What areas need improvement?
- Would they recommend us to others?

How we applied this at Mirabelle:

We introduced real-time feedback requests (quick surveys after check-in, room service, and checkout), implemented Net Promoter Score (NPS) to track how likely guests were to recommend us; we created a guest insights dashboard—analyzing reviews, complaints, and suggestions.

The result led to repeat bookings increasing by 22% because we fixed hidden issues that guests pointed out.

2. Employee Satisfaction: Keep the Team Engaged

- Are employees happy and motivated?
- What challenges do they face daily?
- Are we providing the right support and career growth?

How we applied this at Mirabelle:

We conducted quarterly anonymous employee surveys to assess morale and workload; held monthly one-on-one check-ins, ensuring that employees felt heard and supported; and created an "Employee Success Score", tracking training participation, engagement, and career growth.

The result was that employee turnover dropped by 18% and productivity improved.

3. Supplier and Partner Satisfaction: Strengthen Business Relationships

- Do suppliers feel valued?
- Are we making business partnerships mutually beneficial?
- Are there operational improvements we can make together?

How we applied this at Mirabelle:

We sent bi-annual supplier satisfaction surveys, asking for honest feedback; created regular partnership meetings to ensure we keep track of their expectations; and built a supplier performance and collaboration dashboard, helping us optimize supply chain efficiency.

The result was that our supplier relationships improved, leading to better pricing, faster deliveries, and more reliability.

The Impact: How Measuring Satisfaction Transformed Mirabelle

Measuring satisfaction led to guest loyalty increasing because we responded to their needs; employees felt more engaged, leading to higher service quality; and supplier efficiency improved, reducing costs and delays. One guest, after noticing the personalized service, told me: "Every time I stay here, it feels like Mirabelle just keeps getting better. It's like you actually listen to guests!" That's when I knew measuring satisfaction wasn't just about data; it was about continuous improvement.

Final Lesson: What Gets Measured, Gets Improved

- You can't improve what you don't measure.
- Listening to customers, employees, and partners leads to long-term success.
- A commitment to measuring satisfaction builds trust and loyalty.

At Mirabelle, we don't just serve; we listen, learn, and evolve because the key to success isn't only doing well—it's knowing where to do even better.

Satisfy Relevant Interest Groups

When I first started Mirabelle, I thought success meant making guests happy, but I quickly realized success isn't just about guests—it's about satisfying everyone who plays a role in your business. A thriving business meets the needs of all its key interest groups: customers, employees, partners and suppliers, society, and key decision-makers. That's when I made a commitment: Mirabelle would focus on satisfying every interest group, not just our guests.

The Wake-Up Call: When One Happy Group Wasn't Enough

One season, we had record-high guest satisfaction scores. I was thrilled—until I saw another report: Employee morale was low—they felt overworked; suppliers were frustrated—they weren't getting timely payments; and key decision-makers wanted clearer updates—they didn't fully understand our growth plan.

I had been so focused on guest happiness that I forgot about the people who made the business possible. That's when I realized a truly successful business satisfies all its key interest groups.

How We Ensured Satisfaction Across All Interest Groups

I developed a plan focused on five key groups:

1. Guest Satisfaction: Create Unforgettable Experiences

- Are we exceeding expectations?
- Do guests feel valued and appreciated?
- Are we listening to their feedback?

How we applied this at Mirabelle:

We implemented a guest loyalty program, rewarding repeat visitors with personalized perks; introduced customized stays, remembering guest preferences for future visits; and launched on-demand guest services, so they could request amenities instantly via an app.

The result was that guest retention increased by 25% and referral bookings grew.

2. Employee Satisfaction: Keep the Team Motivated

- Do employees feel valued and supported?

- Are they motivated to provide exceptional service?
- Are we offering career growth opportunities?

How we applied this at Mirabelle:

We increased employee benefits, offering wellness programs and work-life balance support; created a clear career development path with leadership training; and recognized and rewarded outstanding performance with bonuses and public appreciation.

The result was that employee engagement improved and turnover dropped by 20%.

3. Key Decision-Maker Satisfaction: Provide Transparency and Growth

- Are key decision-makers confident in our business direction?
- Are we delivering financial results and sustainable growth?
- Are we communicating our plan effectively?

How we applied this at Mirabelle:

We held quarterly decision-maker meetings, sharing key performance metrics and future plans; ensured financial transparency, providing clear, data-driven reports; and demonstrated a sustainable growth plan, balancing profit with long-term stability.

The result was that trust increased, leading to easier access to funding for expansion.

4. Partner and Supplier Satisfaction: Build Strong Relationships

- Are we treating suppliers with fairness and respect?
- Are payments and orders handled smoothly?
- Are we fostering long-term partnerships?

How we applied this at Mirabelle:

We created clear, long-term contracts, ensuring fair pricing and reliable delivery; improved payment efficiency, so suppliers were always paid on time; and established joint marketing efforts, featuring local vendors in our guest materials.

The result was that supplier reliability improved, and we secured better pricing and priority service.

5. Community and Environmental Responsibility: Give Back

- Are we contributing positively to the local economy?
- Are we minimizing our environmental impact?
- Are we engaged in meaningful community initiatives?

How we applied this at Mirabelle:

We partnered with local artists and businesses, integrating them into our guest experience; adopted eco-friendly initiatives, including waste reduction and energy conservation; and sponsored community events and charities, reinforcing our commitment to social impact.

The result was that the community viewed Mirabelle as a responsible, valued contributor, leading to strong local support.

The Impact: How Multi-Level Satisfaction Transformed Mirabelle

When we focused on multi-level impact at Mirabelle, guests became loyal advocates, returning and referring others; employees stayed longer, leading to better service quality; key decision-makers remained committed, fueling sustainable growth; suppliers prioritized us, strengthening our operations; and the local community embraced us, reinforcing our brand. One key decision-maker told me: "What makes Mirabelle special isn't just the guest experience—it's how you balance success while keeping everyone engaged and satisfied." That's when I knew that true success is about making sure that every interest group benefits.

Final Lesson: Satisfying All Interest Groups Leads to Sustainable Success

- A business that satisfies only one group is at risk.
- Happy employees create better guest experiences.
- Strong relationships with key decision-makers and suppliers drive growth.
- Engaging with the community builds long-term trust and reputation.

At Mirabelle, we don't just focus on one aspect of success; we ensure satisfaction at every level because a balanced business is a thriving business.

Use Feedback to Increase Satisfaction

When I first started Mirabelle, I assumed that as long as we were delivering great service, our interest groups—guests, employees, and partners and suppliers—would be satisfied. But then I realized that what *I* think is great service doesn't matter. What *they* think, does. Feedback isn't just criticism—it's a roadmap to continuous improvement. That's when I made a commitment: Mirabelle would use feedback as a tool to increase satisfaction across all interest groups.

The Wake-Up Call: When We Didn't Listen

One year, we received consistent guest complaints about slow room service delivery. At first, I assumed we needed more employees, guests were being impatient, and the kitchen was too busy. But when we finally analyzed feedback in detail, we found the real problem: Orders were getting delayed because the order notification system wasn't working properly. Employees weren't seeing new requests instantly. Once we fixed it by upgrading our internal communication system, complaints dropped by 80% in one month. That's when I realized feedback is useful only if you act on it.

How We Built a Feedback-Driven Business

To turn feedback into action, I focused on three key areas:

1. Gather Feedback from All Interest Groups

- Are we collecting feedback regularly?
- Are we making it easy for people to share their thoughts?
- Are we receiving feedback from multiple sources?

How we applied this at Mirabelle:

We installed real-time guest feedback stations in the lobby and rooms, conducted monthly employee feedback surveys to understand team concerns, and held quarterly meetings with suppliers and partners to address collaboration challenges.

The result was that we started catching issues before they became big problems.

2. Analyze and Identify Patterns in Feedback

- Are we spotting trends in feedback?
- Are certain complaints or suggestions repeating over time?
- Are we prioritizing the most impactful improvements?

How we applied this at Mirabelle:

We created a feedback tracking dashboard, so we could see common issues at a glance; grouped complaints into categories (e.g., service, amenities, check-in experience); and prioritized changes based on frequency and impact (e.g., fixing Wi-Fi issues affected more guests than changing the coffee brand).

The result was that instead of making random improvements, we focused on what mattered most.

3. Take Action and Communicate Changes

- Are we actually fixing the problems we identify?
- Are we letting people know their feedback made a difference?
- Are we measuring the impact of the changes?

How we applied this at Mirabelle:

We created a "You Spoke, We Listened" campaign, informing guests and employees about improvements based on their feedback; trained managers to personally follow up with guests who left constructive feedback; and conducted before-and-after satisfaction surveys to measure if changes were working.

The result was that guest satisfaction increased by 30% in areas where we made improvements.

One guest told me: "I love that you actually listen to feedback. I complained about the slow check-in last time, and now it's completely seamless. That's why I keep coming back!" That's when I knew feedback wasn't just a tool for fixing problems; it was a plan for creating long-term loyalty.

The Impact: How Feedback Transformed Mirabelle

Once we made transformations based on feedback, guests trusted us more because they saw that their opinions mattered; employees became more engaged because they knew their voices were heard; and our reputation improved, leading to higher ratings and more bookings. Using feedback to constantly refine and improve, we stayed ahead of competitors who were still relying on guesswork.

Final Lesson: Listening Leads to Loyalty

- Collecting feedback is useless unless you act on it.
- The best improvements come from the people who experience your business firsthand.
- Communicating changes builds trust and long-term satisfaction.

At Mirabelle, we don't just listen; we take action because when people see that their feedback matters, they stay with you for life.

Harvest the Fruits of Your Success

For years, I was so focused on growth and improvement at Mirabelle that I never stopped to appreciate our progress. We had happy guests, a strong team, and a profitable, sustainable business. But instead of celebrating these wins, I kept asking: *What's next? How can we improve further? What challenges do we need to overcome?*

Then, one day, a longtime guest pulled me aside and said: "Maya, you've built something truly special here. Do you ever take a moment to enjoy it?" That's when I realized success isn't just about achieving goals—it's about recognizing, celebrating, and enjoying what we've built.

The Wake-Up Call: When I Almost Missed the Moment

One evening, we hosted Mirabelle's 5th anniversary celebration. The lobby was filled with returning guests who loved our hotel, employees who had grown with us, partners and suppliers who helped us succeed, and key decision-makers who believed in our vision.

As I looked around, I felt a deep sense of pride and gratitude. But at the same time, I caught myself thinking: *What should we improve next? Are we maximizing our potential? How do we scale this further?* Then I realized that if I never stop to acknowledge our achievements, success will always feel just out of reach. That night, I made a decision: We would celebrate every win—big and small—because success deserves to be enjoyed.

How We Learned to Recognize and Enjoy Success

I implemented a three-step mindset shift at Mirabelle to ensure that we truly harvested the fruits of our success.

1. Acknowledge and Celebrate Wins

- Do we take time to reflect on what we've accomplished?
- Are we recognizing the people who contributed to our success?
- Do we celebrate progress—not just perfection?

How we applied this at Mirabelle:

We held quarterly "Success Reflection" meetings, where we reviewed our wins and progress; we publicly recognized top-performing employees, rewarding their contributions; and we shared success stories with guests and partners, showing the impact of our work.

The result was that employees felt more motivated and guests connected more deeply with our brand.

2. Enjoy the Success, Not Just Chase the Next Goal

- Are we allowing ourselves to experience joy in our achievements?
- Do we take time to reflect on how far we've come?
- Are we balancing ambition with appreciation?

How we applied this at Mirabelle:

We started blocking time every month to reflect on personal and business milestones; we created a Wall of Achievements in the hotel, highlighting key moments in our journey; and we hosted annual "success dinners" for our team, guests, and partners to celebrate together.

The result was that we stopped seeing success as just a stepping stone—we started experiencing it.

3. Reinforce Success by Giving Back

- Are we using our success to create a bigger impact?
- Are we sharing our knowledge and experience with others?
- Are we ensuring that our success is meaningful and lasting?

How we applied this at Mirabelle:

We launched a mentorship program, helping new entrepreneurs in the hospitality industry; invested in community projects, reinvesting a portion of profits into local sustainability efforts; and created a "Mirabelle Alumni Network", connecting past employees and partners to foster long-term relationships.

The result was that success became bigger than just us; it became something that positively influenced others.

The Impact: How Enjoying Success Made Us Even Stronger

When we celebrated and enjoyed our wins, employees felt more valued and motivated, guests connected with our brand on a deeper level, we maintained long-term partnerships because of shared success, and our reputation grew, attracting even more opportunities. One employee told me: "I've never worked somewhere that actually celebrates wins. It makes me want to give my best every day." That's when I knew harvesting success isn't about stopping growth; it's about appreciating the journey.

Final Lesson: Success Isn't Just About Reaching Goals—It's About Enjoying Them

- Recognizing success keeps you motivated.
- Celebrating wins strengthens relationships.
- Sharing success creates lasting impact.
- A business that enjoys its success attracts more success.

At Mirabelle, we don't just strive for success; we take the time to celebrate, reflect, and give back—because true success is meant to be enjoyed.

Be Proud of Your Success

For years, I believed that humility and constant improvement were the keys to success at Mirabelle. I always looked for ways to improve, focused on what was next, and avoided celebrating too much, thinking it might slow us down. But then I realized something important: If you don't take pride in your success, no one else will. Being proud of what we've built isn't about arrogance—it's about recognizing the journey, the hard work, and the impact we've made.

The Wake-Up Call: When I Didn't See What We Had Built

One evening, I walked through Mirabelle's lobby and overheard a guest talking to a friend: "This is my favorite hotel. They just do things differently. It feels like home." I smiled, but my mind immediately went to: *We still have things to improve. The expansion project isn't finished yet, and we could be doing more.* That's when I realized I was so focused on what was missing that I wasn't appreciating what we had already achieved. Success doesn't just come from striving for more—it comes from recognizing how far you've come. That day, I made a promise to myself that I would start being proud of our success—not just chasing the next milestone.

How We Started Owning Our Success

I implemented a three-step approach to help myself and the Mirabelle team take pride in what we had built.

1. Reflect on Accomplishments—Big and Small

- Are we acknowledging milestones, not just chasing new goals?
- Do we remind ourselves how far we've come?
- Are we taking time to appreciate our journey?

How we applied this at Mirabelle:

We created a "Success Timeline Wall", displaying key moments in our growth; we held quarterly reflection meetings, where we reviewed our biggest wins; and we started a "Proud Moments" initiative, where employees shared stories of their favorite achievements.

The result was that everyone felt a deeper connection to the business. It wasn't just a job, it was a shared achievement.

2. Share Success Stories with the World

- Are we telling our story with pride?
- Are we inspiring others with our journey?
- Are we letting guests, employees, and partners feel like part of something bigger?

How we applied this at Mirabelle:

We started featuring "Behind the Brand" stories highlighting our journey in social media and marketing; we encouraged employees to share their own success stories, celebrating promotions, milestones, and breakthroughs; and we partnered with travel publications, sharing our sustainability efforts and unique hospitality approach.

The result was that our brand reputation grew and guests felt even more connected to our story.

3. Lead with Confidence—Own Our Success

- Are we proud of what we've built, or do we downplay it?
- Do we stand behind our achievements with confidence?
- Are we inspiring our team, partners, and guests through our leadership?

How we applied this at Mirabelle:

We stopped saying "we're just a small boutique hotel"; instead, we owned our identity as an industry leader in personalized hospitality; we celebrated team wins publicly, ensuring that employees knew their efforts mattered; and I personally learned to speak about our success with pride, instead of always focusing on "what's next".

The result was that confidence attracted bigger opportunities, better partnerships, and long-term loyalty.

The Impact: How Taking Pride in Success Transformed Mirabelle

Once we began taking pride in our success transformation, employees became more motivated—knowing their hard work was part of something special; guests felt emotionally connected to our journey, making them more loyal; our reputation grew—people saw us as a leader, not just another hotel; and partners and suppliers wanted to collaborate more, strengthening our business network.

One of our longest-serving employees told me: "Maya, I've always loved working here, but now I realize we've built something truly amazing. I'm proud to be a part of Mirabelle." That's when I knew success isn't just about what we achieve; it's about how we embrace and share it.

Final Lesson: Success Should Be Celebrated, Not Just Chased

- Recognizing your achievements doesn't mean you stop growing.
- Confidence in your success attracts more opportunities.
- Sharing your journey builds deeper connections with employees, partners and suppliers, and customers.
- Pride in what you've built fuels motivation for the future.

At Mirabelle, we don't just build success; we own it, celebrate it, and inspire others with it because success is meant to be lived with pride.

Secure Your Existence in the Future

When I first opened Mirabelle, I was focused on daily operations and short-term success: Keeping guests happy, managing finances efficiently, and growing our reputation. But then I asked myself: *What happens five years from now? Ten years? Will Mirabelle still be thriving, or will we struggle to keep up?* That's when I realized success today means nothing if you don't prepare for tomorrow, and the only way to secure long-term success is through the continuous and consistent application of KAIZUNO.

KAIZUNO isn't just about improving what's broken; it's about proactively securing the future by evolving, adapting, and staying ahead of change. A business that applies KAIZUNO once will see short-term success; a business that applies KAIZUNO consistently and continuously will secure its future.

The Wake-Up Call: When I Almost Got Left Behind

One year, a new luxury hotel chain opened up nearby. They had cutting-edge technology (AI-powered concierge, automated room controls), a modern, eco-friendly design, and an aggressive marketing that attracted our audience.

I assumed guests would stay loyal to Mirabelle, but soon I noticed our bookings started slowing down, some of our repeat guests wanted "a fresher experience", and we weren't as competitive as we thought. That's when I realized the hospitality industry was changing fast and if we didn't evolve, we'd be left behind. From that moment on, I made a commitment that Mirabelle wouldn't just exist; we would secure our future through the consistent and continuous implementation of KAIZUNO.

How We Used KAIZUNO to Secure Our Future

I focused on three core KAIZUNO principles to ensure Mirabelle's long-term success:

1. Adapt and Continuously Improve Based on Trends

- Are we keeping up with industry shifts?
- Are we proactively listening to what future guests will want?
- Are we improving in a structured, ongoing way?

How we applied KAIZUNO at Mirabelle:

We invested in smart hotel technology—automated check-ins, voice-controlled rooms, and AI-driven guest preferences; expanded our wellness and sustainability offerings, responding to rising demand for eco-conscious travel; and developed a "Future Guest Experience" taskforce, constantly researching and testing new trends.

The result was that we positioned ourselves as a forward-thinking, modern brand—not just another hotel.

2. Build Financial Stability and Long-Term Profitability

- Do we have the financial strength to survive economic downturns?
- Are we diversifying revenue streams?
- Are we reinvesting profits into future growth?

How we applied KAIZUNO at Mirabelle:

We created a financial risk management plan, ensuring that we had cash reserves for unexpected challenges; diversified revenue by offering subscription-based VIP memberships, exclusive long-stay packages, and corporate partnerships; and reinvested a portion of profits into innovation, ensuring continuous upgrades and improvements.

The result was that we became financially resilient, able to weather challenges without cutting quality or service.

3. Strengthen Brand Loyalty and Community Engagement

- Are we building a brand that people will stay connected to?
- Are we engaging with our community for long-term relevance?
- Are we creating meaningful partnerships that reinforce our business?

How we applied KAIZUNO at Mirabelle:

We launched a guest loyalty program with unique, personalized rewards; invested in community engagement projects, hosting local cultural events and sustainability initiatives; and partnered with influential travel brands and local businesses, creating a strong network of support.

The result was that guests felt emotionally connected to Mirabelle, making us their first choice in the future.

The Impact: How KAIZUNO Secured Mirabelle's Future

When we implemented the KAIZUNO principles, we stayed ahead of competitors, maintaining our reputation as an industry leader; our revenue streams became more stable, ensuring long-term financial health; and guests, employees, and partners remained loyal, creating a strong foundation for sustained success. One of our longest-standing guests told me: "Every time I come back, Mirabelle feels fresh, modern, and ahead of the curve. I never have to look for another hotel." That's when I knew we weren't just running a hotel; we were securing our existence through KAIZUNO consistently and continuously.

Final Lesson: KAIZUNO = Long-Term Success

- Survival isn't enough—businesses must evolve and innovate to stay relevant.
- Financial stability ensures that you can invest in the future, not just survive the present.

- A strong brand and loyal community create long-term success.
- KAIZUNO must be applied consistently and continuously to secure the future.

At Mirabelle, we don't just exist today; we are building a future where we thrive—because KAIZUNO guarantees that true success lasts beyond the present.

Final Reflection of Maya Dani

As I walked off the stage, the applause faded into the background, but one thought remained clear in my mind. For years, I had believed success was about getting everything right—about having the perfect plan, the perfect timing, the perfect execution. But I had been wrong. Success isn't about perfection; it's about clarity, adaptability, balance, and consistency. It's about stepping forward even when you're uncertain, turning failures into lessons, and leading with conviction—even when no one else sees the vision. Mirabelle wasn't built on luck; it was built on structured, deliberate action. And that action followed a simple yet powerful approach: **KAIZUNO.**

STEP 1: Strive for Success—Everything starts with a clear purpose. I had to define what success meant—not just profits, but creating an unforgettable experience for every guest who walked through our doors. Without a vision, success is just a moving target.

STEP 2: Thrive Through Relationships—Business is never built alone. I had to surround myself with the right people—my team, my suppliers, my guests. Every successful journey is a shared effort.

STEP 3: Embrace Balanced Planning—A dream without a plan is just a wish. I learned that rigid planning kills innovation, but balanced planning empowers action. I designed a plan that was structured yet flexible, allowing us to adapt and grow.

STEP 4: Pursue Practical Implementation—Ideas don't build businesses, actions do. We moved fast, tested our strategies, and adjusted as needed. Perfection isn't the goal, progress is.

STEP 5: Secure Sustainable Success—Mirabelle wasn't just about me. To build something that lasts, I had to think beyond today. By embedding a strong culture of growth and continuous improvement, Mirabelle became more than just a hotel—it became a legacy.

These five STEPS turned a forgotten building into a thriving business, and KAIZUNO made this possible.

I turned back for a final glance at the audience—hundreds of eyes watching, some filled with inspiration, others with determination. Maybe some of them would leave tonight and start their own journey. Maybe, somewhere out there, another forgotten building was waiting for its second chance.

I smiled, encouraging the audience to: Dream big. Start now. Apply KAIZUNO. And, keep going.

And with that, I stepped forward—ready for the next chapter of my life, knowing that whatever that chapter may be, the KAIZUNO method would be there to help.

Start Your KAIZUNO Journey

Congratulations! You've completed a journey seeing KAIZUNO in action; but this is just the beginning. Now, it's time for you to take action:

Apply what you've learned—start small and build momentum.

Engage with the KAIZUNO community—connect with others who are using the same framework.

Track your progress—use the KAIZUNO STEPS to refine and improve your approach.

Share your success—help others by sharing how KAIZUNO has impacted your journey.

Your success story starts today. Keep striving, thriving, and securing your future with KAIZUNO!

KAIZUNO Team Contact Information

Do you want to apply our KAIZUNO digital services and need professional help?

We have developed the first AI-powered digital KAIZUNO system on the basis of the 5 STEPS.

KAIZUNO combines cutting-edge AI with proven methodologies to help organizations, teams, and leaders achieve rapid and sustainable improvements.

- **AI-driven insights**—Gain real-time clarity on strengths, challenges, and opportunities.
- **3x more successful, 10x faster, 80% time & cost savings and efficient**—Achieve success more efficiently than conventional approaches.
- **Custom-tailored guidance**—Adapt to any industry, organization, or growth phase.
- **Engage your team**—Ensure clarity, accountability, and long-term results.

With our digital system, you see the full potential of KAIZUNO. You want to use it as your digital companion and apply it for your whole organization, parts of it, specific perspectives, or just for a project. Anytime, quick and simple.

Now is the time to take action.

If you need tailored professional support…

If you are looking for structured, AI-driven guidance…

If you want to ensure long-term, measurable success…

Connect with us today and take the next step.

Website: www.kaizuno.com

LinkedIn: https://www.linkedin.com/company/kaizuno

About the Authors

Dr. Christian Forstner is a distinguished scientist and consultant with over 30 years of experience in supporting organizations to enhance their competitive advantage and sustainable success. After extensive academic work in international research teams and many years in a very large, complex, and international industrial environment, Christian discovered the simple **KAIZUNO** approach like a natural law some 20 years ago. His discovery was based on the fundamental insight that complex systems can be most effectively understood, managed, and optimized with simple approaches.

Having spent many years in leadership roles at Siemens, Christian founded CF YOUR ADVANTAGE: https://cfyouradvantage.com/ to fully pursue his passion for driving organizational excellence. His sector experience includes automotive, energy, industry, banking, healthcare, national authorities, transport and logistics, telecommunications, security, defense, oil and gas, food, research, social welfare work, and education. His work has taken him across Europe, Turkey, China, India, Japan, Africa, USA, and many Arab nations, providing him with a rich understanding of diverse cultural and organizational contexts.

As an excellence consultant, Christian has supported, assessed, and developed numerous organizations of any size and nature worldwide, offering expertise in strategy, leadership, process and risk management, sustainability, and many other fields of competence. Christian is the co-founder of Excellence Talks, the world's largest community for business excellence.

Murat Aydin is a recognized leader in operational and business excellence, quality management, and regulatory compliance. With over 17 years of experience in strategic consulting and executive leadership, he has supported organizations across various industries in transformation, process optimization, regulatory compliance, and achieving sustainable top performance.

As a co-founder of Excellence Talks, the world's largest community for business excellence with half a million followers, he brings together decision-makers, subject matter experts, and companies. Through Excellence Talks and other platforms, he fosters the exchange of excellence, innovation, and best practices, significantly shaping the evolution of this field.

In addition to his cross-industry consulting work, he is the co-founder of Excellence Squad (XSQ), a consulting firm dedicated exclusively to the life sciences sector. XSQ helps pharmaceutical, biotechnology, and medical device companies navigate quality and regulatory challenges, operational transformations, and business excellence initiatives.

His career includes leadership positions at Unilever and GC Europe. During his tenure at GC Europe, he led profound transformations that contributed to the company winning the EFQM Global Excellence Award in 2019—a historic achievement for the medical technology industry and a subsidiary of a Japanese corporation.

With a strong academic foundation—a Bachelor in Engineering, a Master of Engineering in Technical Management, and an Executive MBA from Vlerick Business School, Murat combines deep expertise with practical implementation.

Murat's focus areas include continuous improvement (Kaizen), innovation management, transformation, project management, sustainability, supply chain management, quality assurance, and compliance—crucial factors for organizations striving to embed excellence as a principle of success.

Dr. Robert Knop is a seasoned strategist, investor, and digital transformation leader, dedicated to making business excellence both accessible and actionable. His career spans strategy consulting at Accenture, where he led global transformation projects, to private equity, where he evaluated over 100 companies and took on leadership roles as CEO, CMO, and CIO to drive operational success. His deep understanding of aligning people, processes, technology, and financial resources stems from firsthand experience in guiding businesses through complex change.

As a board member of ESPRIX Excellence Suisse, Robert actively shapes Switzerland's competitive landscape, conducting business excellence assessments across Europe, the Middle East, and Asia. At Zühlke Engineering, he spearheaded the digital transformation unit, helping companies develop pragmatic, business-driven solutions in industries ranging from energy to security. His collaboration with the Swiss Chamber of Commerce (WIBS) further demonstrates his commitment to making digital transformation practical for SMEs.

Academically, Robert holds a doctorate in strategic networks of SMEs, an MBA from California State University, and a business administration diploma, all with highest honors. His expertise culminates in KAIZUNO, a groundbreaking methodology and platform co-developed with select collaborators. Combining business excellence principles with intuitive digital tools, KAIZUNO represents the integration of his strategic, operational, and technological insights—helping organizations navigate change, engage their teams, and achieve sustainable success.